THE

MEDIEVAL

CATHEDRAL

TITLES IN THE BUILDING HISTORY SERIES INCLUDE:

Alcatraz

The Eiffel Tower

The Great Wall of China

The Medieval Castle

The Medieval Cathedral

Mount Rushmore

The New York Subway System

The Palace of Versailles

The Panama Canal

The Parthenon of Ancient Greece

The Pyramids of Giza

The Roman Colosseum

Roman Roads and Aqueducts

Shakespeare's Globe

The Sistine Chapel

Stonehenge

The Titanic

The Transcontinental Railroad

The Viking Longship

The White House

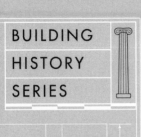
THE
MEDIEVAL
CATHEDRAL

by William W. Lace

Lucent Books, Inc., San Diego, California

JY 24 01

Library of Congress Cataloging-in-Publication Data

Lace, William W.
    The medieval cathedral / by William W. Lace.
        p.   cm. — (Building history series)
    Includes bibliographical references (p.) and index.
    ISBN 1-56006-720-9 (hardcover)
    1. Architecture, Medieval—Europe—Juvenile literature.
2. Architecture, Gothic—Europe—Juvenile literature. 3. Cathedrals—
Europe—Design and construction—Juvenile literature.
[1. Cathedrals. 2. Architecture, Gothic. 3. Civilization, Medieval.]
I. Title.   II. Series.
  NA5453 .L33 2001
  726.6'4'0940902—dc21

                                                            00-010083

Copyright 2001 by Lucent Books, Inc.
P.O. Box 289011, San Diego, California, 92198-9011

                    Printed in the U.S.A.

CONTENTS

FOREWORD

Throughout history, as civilizations have evolved and prospered, each has produced unique buildings and architectural styles. Combining the need for both utility and artistic expression, a society's buildings, particularly its large-scale public structures, often reflect the individual character traits that distinguish it from other societies. In a very real sense, then, buildings express a society's values and unique characteristics in tangible form. As scholar Anita Abramovitz comments in her book *People and Spaces*, "Our ways of living and thinking—our habits, needs, fear of enemies, aspirations, materialistic concerns, and religious beliefs—have influenced the kinds of spaces that we build and that later surround and include us."

That specific types and styles of structures constitute an outward expression of the spirit of an individual people or era can be seen in the diverse ways that various societies have built palaces, fortresses, tombs, churches, government buildings, sports arenas, public works, and other such monuments. The ancient Greeks, for instance, were a supremely rational people who originated Western philosophy and science, including the atomic theory and the realization that the earth is a sphere. Their public buildings, epitomized by Athens's magnificent Parthenon temple, were equally rational, emphasizing order, harmony, reason, and above all, restraint.

By contrast, the Romans, who conquered and absorbed the Greek lands, were a highly practical people preoccupied with acquiring and wielding power over others. The Romans greatly admired and readily copied elements of Greek architecture, but modified and adapted them to their own needs. "Roman genius was called into action by the enormous practical needs of a world empire," wrote historian Edith Hamilton. "Rome met them magnificently. Buildings tremendous, indomitable, amphitheaters where eighty thousand could watch a spectacle, baths where three thousand could bathe at the same time."

In medieval Europe, God heavily influenced and motivated the people, and religion permeated all aspects of society, molding people's worldviews and guiding their everyday actions. That spiritual mindset is reflected in the most important medieval structure—the Gothic cathedral—which, in a sense, was a model of heavenly cities. As scholar Anne Fremantle so elegantly phrases it, the cathedrals were "harmonious elevations of stone and glass reaching up to heaven to seek and receive the light [of God]."

Our more secular modern age, in contrast, is driven by the realities of a global economy, advanced technology, and mass communications. Responding to the needs of international trade and the growth of cities housing millions of people, today's builders construct engineering marvels, among them towering skyscrapers of steel and glass, mammoth marine canals, and huge and elaborate rapid transit systems, all of which would have left their ancestors, even the Romans, awestruck.

In examining some of humanity's greatest edifices, Lucent Books' Building History series recognizes this close relationship between a society's historical character and its buildings. Each volume in the series begins with a historical sketch of the people who erected the edifice, exploring their major achievements as well as the beliefs, customs, and societal needs that dictated the variety, functions, and styles of their buildings. A detailed explanation of how the selected structure was conceived, designed, and built, to the extent that this information is known, makes up the majority of the volume.

Each volume in the Lucent Building History series also includes several special features that are useful tools for additional research. A chronology of important dates gives students an overview, at a glance, of the evolution and use of the structure described. Sidebars create a broader context by adding further details on some of the architects, engineers, and construction tools, materials, and methods that made each structure a reality, as well as the social, political, and/or religious leaders and movements that inspired its creation. Useful maps help the reader locate the nations, cities, streets, and individual structures mentioned in the text; and numerous diagrams and pictures illustrate tools and devices that bring to life various stages of construction. Finally, each volume contains two bibliographies, one for student research, the other listing works the author consulted in compiling the book.

Taken as a whole, these volumes, covering diverse ancient and modern structures, constitute not only a valuable research tool, but also a tribute to the human spirit, a fascinating exploration of the dreams, skills, ingenuity, and dogged determination of the great peoples who shaped history.

IMPORTANT DATES IN THE BUILDING OF THE MEDIEVAL CATHEDRAL

476
Germanic invaders depose the last emperor of Rome; the Dark Ages begin.

313
Emperor Constantine legalizes Christianity throughout the Roman Empire.

ca. 70
Christians in Rome worship in underground catacombs.

ca. 1119
Bernard becomes abbot of Cistercian monastery at Clairvaux in France.

ca. 1130
Cistercian churches are built in accordance with geometric forms.

1162
Rebuilding of the cathedral of Notre Dame in Paris Begins

1194
Rebuilding of t Chartres Cathe begins in Fran

70 | 300 | 500 | 1000 | 1150 | 1200

ca. 350
Christian churches are built in the basilica style.

ca. 400
Transepts are developed to seat additional clergy; arched roofs are used to increase the size of churches.

ca. 1000
Romanesque style of building begins.

1137–1144
Abbot Suger builds the first Gothic church at Saint-Denis in France.

1165
Building of the Choir of Reims Cathedral begins in France.

1174
Building of the Canterbury Cathedral begins in England.

1192
Building of the Choir of Lincoln Cathedral begins in England.

1309
Papacy is moved from Rome to Avignon, France.

1220
The foundation stone is laid for the Amiens Cathedral in France.

1319–1339
St. Ouen in France is built in the Rayonnant style.

1339
Hundred Years' War breaks out between England and France.

1200	1300	1400	1500	1600

1349–1351
Black Death sweeps Europe killing one-fourth to one-third of the population.

1365
Strasbourg Cathedral in Germany is finished in the Flamboyant style.

1543
Building of the Louvre palace begins in the Renaissance style.

1231
Rebuilding of Saint-Denis begins.

1229
Rebuilding of the York Cathedral begins in England.

INTRODUCTION

Throughout the centuries, the medieval cathedrals of western Europe have dominated all that surrounds them. The buildings erected by subsequent generations may be larger, taller, and more opulent, but none can match the grandeur of these soaring expressions of faith.

Many cathedrals that once towered over only rude houses of timber and mud now stand amidst the swirl of metropolitan capitals. They remain somehow apart from the modern world that ebbs and flows around them, standing timeless and eternal. To enter them is to leave today behind. The discordant clamor of the city fades and then disappears with every step down the broad central aisle. The harsh sunlight is muted, softened as it is filtered through stained glass windows high above.

This is the world of the cathedral builders and others who lived, worked, and worshiped in these great churches. The medieval cathedral was a product of the Middle Ages, the time— from which the word *medieval* derives—roughly between 1100 and 1400. It was a world very different from today's, not only in how people lived but also in how they thought.

AN AGE OF PIETY

Life was harsh and often cruel, and people turned to God for consolation. The age of reason, in which humanity began to discover scientific causes for natural phenomena, lay far in the future. In the medieval mind, the world was explained in terms of faith. God, the great creator, was at the center of all things. The cosmos was an orderly pyramid with God at the pinnacle and humanity at the bottom. Life on Earth was but a brief, transitory stop. Heaven and hell were very close and very real, not mere abstractions.

Christianity was the central controlling authority of western Europe. Nations, in the modern sense, had not yet developed. People thought of themselves not as residents of France or England, but rather of Christendom. The church was supreme, and even the greatest kings bowed to the will of popes.

AN AGE OF SUPERSTITION

It was an age of superstition as well. Witches, demons, and monsters were much more than fairy-tale characters. Christian beliefs had not yet outlived the relics of a pagan past. Even so, the medieval world was one of change and progress. Universities were founded in which scholars pondered the nature of God and the universe. Literature began to flourish after languishing throughout the so-called Dark Ages since the fall of Rome. The

Cathedrals such as Notre Dame in Paris remain apart from the modern world, standing timeless and eternal.

Crusades brought Europe in touch with other civilizations, thus introducing both new ideas and new consumer goods. Trade began to blossom as did wealth. Towns prospered, and a new merchant class was born.

This medieval world, with its boundless faith and energetic spirit, found an ultimate expression in the cathedral. Just as men sought to rise above earthly matters and attain a higher spiritual plane, these remarkable buildings seemed to leap from the ground, reaching up as if seeking heaven. God was all-powerful, and these were God's houses. To be sure, they were objects of enormous civil pride, but they were built primarily as testaments of faith, as offerings of love and obedience. "Non nobis, sed tibi, Domine," vowed the cathedral builders. "Not for us, but for Thee, O God."

THE CHRISTIAN HERITAGE

To the people of the time, the medieval cathedral must have seemed like a miracle. Even though they may have personally labored on its construction, cutting timber and hauling stone, it was as if this soaring expression of Christian faith sprang from the very mind of God, who guided the hands of the builders. Actually, however, the medieval cathedral was the product of more than a thousand years of both religious and architectural evolution.

When Jesus of Nazareth was crucified in about A.D. 33, Christianity almost died with him. This religion, later to become

This fifteenth-century painting depicts the crucifixion of Jesus of Nazareth, an act that almost spelled the end of Christianity.

the dominant force of medieval Europe, was kept alive only because a handful of followers in Palestine were willing to risk
sharing their leader's fate in order to spread his teachings. Condemned as heretics by Jewish leaders, and hunted by Roman
soldiers, they met secretly in private homes to worship.

These earliest Christians had no priests, bishops, or churches,
at least in terms of buildings. They were a simple community of
the faithful, led by those who had been Jesus' disciples. As part
of their ritual, they gathered around a table to share bread and
wine, symbolizing the sacrifice of Jesus' body and blood. Thus,
just as the altars of the Jewish and pagan temples throughout
history had been places of sacrifice, so the table bearing the symbols of Jesus' sacrifice became the Christian altar.

The important difference between the early Christian altar
and those preceding it was that no priest conducted the ceremony
as an intermediary between God and the people. Instead, partic-
ipation in the Christian ritual was as a community, hence the term
communion used today to describe it. The idea of community
worship had a major influence on church architecture.

THE CATACOMBS

Christian churches, however, were still far in the future. After
the Roman invasion of Palestine in A.D. 70, the center of activity
shifted to Rome. Christians were no safer there than they had
been in Jerusalem. They met in underground caves called catacombs. The bodies of those who were killed because of their
faith were buried in tombs carved out of the catacomb walls.
These martyrs became the first saints, and the recessed *cubicula*
containing their tombs were the first chapels at which people
worshiped in their memory. From this came the practice of nam-
ing churches after saints and either placing the altar over their
place of burial or placing within the altar a relic of the saint—a
bone, lock of hair, or even a sandal. For much of the Christian
Church's early history no church building or altar could be consecrated, or blessed, unless it held a body or a relic.

After the Edict of Milan in 313, by which Emperor Constantine made Christianity legal throughout his empire, worship was
freed from the darkness of the catacombs. Large buildings were
needed to hold the hundreds of new followers. "Who can number the churches in every town?"[1] wrote Eusebius of Caesarea,
a church historian who died in 340.

Roman soldiers seize a Christian who was practicing his religion in secret in underground caves called catacombs.

BASILICA CHURCHES

The early Christian builders rejected the traditional model of the temple in which the deity was thought to dwell in a secluded inner shrine into which only priests could go. Instead, Christian worship remained a communal act, although by this time a hierarchy of priests and bishops had been established. Church builders instead chose as their model the Roman basilica, or law court.

The basilica, whose style the Romans had copied from ancient Greece, was part of the forum of every Roman city. Outside the basilica was a large marketplace. Inside, the basilica was large and open, so that all citizens could witness the court proceedings. The building was rectangular, about twice as long as it was wide. At the end opposite the door was a semicircular recess known as the apse. In the center of the apse was a cathedra, or

The ruins of the Basilica of Pompeii. The Roman basilica, part of the forum of every Roman city, served as a law court.

throne, from which the Roman judge dispensed justice. As the basilica was transformed into a church, the cathedra became the bishop's throne. Technically, therefore, for a church to be accurately called a cathedral it must be the headquarters of a bishop or archbishop.

Priests sat on either side of the bishop, and the altar was between the bishop and the congregation, usually on a raised platform and situated over the body of a saint. Early altars were bare of decoration and displayed only the plate and chalice used for communion. A ciborium, or canopy, usually hung over the altar, however, proclaiming its holiness. The entire area—apse and altar—was called the chancel, derived from the term *cancelli*, which was a low divider that in Roman times separated the judge and his assistants from the public. At first, the chancel contained only the clergy and altar. Later, singers were installed on either side of the aisle between the altar and the chancel rail, and their area became the choir.

THE NAVE

The large area in which the congregation stood or knelt—chairs or pews would not be used until after the Middle Ages—was called the nave. It was usually divided into aisles—a large center aisle and two side aisles—by rows of columns used to support the roof. Only baptized Christians were permitted in the nave, and at the end of the church opposite the apse was a screened-off foyer called the narthex which acted as a buffer between the church and the area outside the church.

Women were not admitted to the nave, even if they were baptized into the church. The early church followed the example of Eastern religions, including Judaism, and segregated the sexes. Instead of joining the men on the floor of the nave, women were placed in galleries above and to each side. These galleries were called triforia because of their triple openings onto the nave.

Outside the narthex, in what was formerly a marketplace, was the atrium, an open area surrounded by columns in which the unbaptized could receive instruction. In the center of the atrium was the Fountain of Ablution in which church members and converts could wash their hands, much as in more ancient times when a ritual cleansing was required before entering a temple.

TRANSEPTS

The first change in the basic basilica church design came when the church grew, not in terms of the congregation but of the clergy. In the late 300s taxes were extremely heavy as the Roman Empire sought to defend itself from the increasingly powerful "barbarian" tribes outside of its borders. As Zosimus, a historian of the time, explains,

> As the fatal time [to pay taxes] approached all the towns were in grief and tears; the scourge [whip] and rack were used against those whose extreme poverty could not support the tax. Mothers sold their children, and fathers prostituted their daughters, obliged to obtain, by this sorry trade, the money which the tax collectors came to snatch from them.[2]

The Abbey of Maria Laach atrium in Germany.

Under Roman law, priests, both Christian and in the temples of the old gods, were exempt from taxes. Therefore, when the

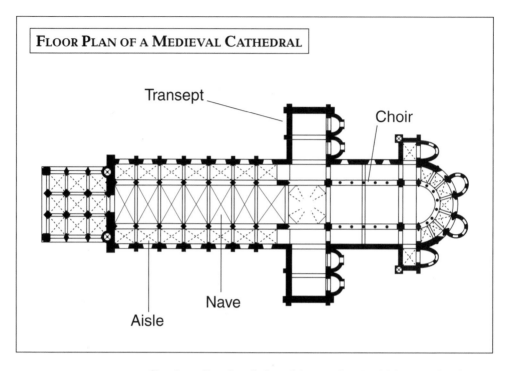

FLOOR PLAN OF A MEDIEVAL CATHEDRAL

Transept

Choir

Aisle

Nave

emperor Gratian dissolved the old temples in 382, a rush of men sought ordination as Christian priests. So great was the increase in the ranks of the clergy that there was no room for them in the apse. To provide more seating, wings, called transepts, were built on each side of the chancel. The addition of transepts had symbolic value as well since it gave churches the shape of a cross.

As the churches expanded in size, they outgrew the basilica style. In these churches roofs were flat and supported by beams, first wooden and then stone, which rested on pillars that, in order to bear the weight of the roof, could not be spaced too far apart. As interior space grew, the number of pillars necessary was such that they interfered with the congregation's ability both to see and hear the service. An architectural technique was needed that would permit a wide central space. The answer was the arch.

USE OF THE ARCH

Arches were not new. They had been used for centuries throughout the Mediterranean, primarily in the Middle East but also in Rome as in the Colosseum and in the huge aqueducts that carried water to the city. Now, forced to bridge large interior spaces, architects began to break free of the classical styles of Greece and Rome.

The advantage of an arched roof over a flat one was that instead of weight pressing straight down on a beam, it could be directed outward and down the sides of the arch to the point where it could shift to a pillar or wall. By using arches, builders reduced the need for pillars. The aisles of the nave, especially the large central aisles, became wider and the entire interior more open.

With the use of arches, churches escaped the restrictions of classical architecture and began to grow both wider and higher. Stone increasingly replaced wood as the primary construction material since arches were able to handle the greater weight. A stone roof had the obvious advantage of lessening the danger of fire.

Even though arches made stone roofs possible, the weight of the roofs was such that walls became thicker and stronger. There were other reasons, however, why churches became more massive. As the number of churches grew, the demand

Arches were not new to cathedral builders; they had been used for centuries in buildings such as the Roman Colosseum.

THE POWER OF RELICS

Ever since some of the earliest Christians prayed at the tombs of those who had given their lives for their faith, relics—be they bones, hair, clothing, or other mementos— of the saints have been an integral part of churches. Through the first few centuries, all churches, in order to be consecrated, had to have under their altars a holy relic.

Many Christians, then and now, believe that saints have the power to intercede with God on their behalf. Thus, relics became objects of power and veneration. In some cases, they were said to have healing powers.

In the Dark Ages, however, with Christianity under attack, other powers—such as the power to punish— were attributed to relics. Historian H. C. Lea, as quoted in *The Heritage of the Cathedral* by Sartell Prentice, describes how priests, essentially defenseless against barbarian attack, turned to relics for protection.

Children are brought to the altar so they can be in the presence of church relics.

Thus there sprang up a luxuriant growth of miraculous interpretations of Providence to vindicate the respect due to the Church and to punish the despoiler of her goods. In fact, the manufacture of these miracles became a recognized armory to which, for centuries, the Church was accustomed to resort. They formed part of the education of the people, who were taught to look with awe upon the priest and his church with their assortment of relics; upon the monastery with its tempting vineyards, orchard, apiaries [honey bee colonies], and fields of grain; upon the Episcopal palace and cathedral with their treasures accumulated from the piety of generations. The unarmed Churchman could ill guard, by force, the rich possessions entrusted to his care, and if he busied himself with imagining and disseminating the marvels which proved that his person and his property were the peculiar [special] care of God, we should not too sternly judge and condemn him.

for relics grew. Not only did relics commemorate saints, but they also increasingly were thought to have healing powers. They became the most valuable objects in a church as well as in an entire city. As Rome's power decreased and the threat of barbarian invasions grew, a constant state of warfare existed on the empire's borders. It was not uncommon for relics to be seized as spoils of victory by Christian and non-Christian enemies. Churches, therefore, became more like fortresses.

INTERIOR CHANGES

The increased importance of relics had an effect on the interior arrangement of churches as well. As if retreating from an increasingly hostile world, the main altar was pushed back into the end of the apse. The bishop's throne was now between the altar and the congregation, and he celebrated communion with his back toward the people, thus departing further from the communal aspect of the Christian ceremony.

Not satisfied with a single relic under or contained in the main altar, churches collected additional relics and built individual shrines to each of them. These altars were placed in niches around the apse on either side of the main altar. The aisle that curved in front of them was called the ambulatory since it carried a flow of pilgrims from shrine to shrine. Additional shrines were built into the walls of the transepts.

The atrium was another victim of the troubled times. As churches became places of refuge as well as of worship, unbaptized persons were admitted to seek both physical safety and spiritual guidance. The atrium, now both unnecessary and vulnerable, moved inside the walls of the church property and became the cloister—an open area to which the clergy could retreat for meditation.

TOWERS

When the atrium, with its attractive columns, disappeared, some sort of architectural element was needed to relieve the blank face of the entrance wall. The solution, one both practical and attractive, were towers built on each side of the entrance. On one hand, they served the dual purposes of housing the bells used to call the faithful to services and of furnishing a vantage point from

The cloister of Notre Dame in Le Puy. Cloisters are open areas to which the clergy could retreat for meditation.

which to spot approaching danger. On the other, they developed from squat, flat-roofed structures into the magnificent spires of the medieval cathedral.

At last the Roman Empire in the west—the eastern part was ruled from Byzantium, or modern-day Istanbul, Turkey—fell before successive invasions of Germanic tribes. The last emperor, Romulus Augustus, was deposed in 476, and Europe entered the Dark Ages. Learning declined, and the skills that church architects had inherited from their Greek and Roman predecessors were lost. Little progress was made during most of the next five hundred years.

THE NEW MILLENNIUM

In the year 1000, however, an amazing thing happened—or rather, did not happen. Christian Europe had been battered by centuries of invasions by non-Christians, particularly Vikings in the north, Islamic Moors in the south, and Magyars in the east. During the years when it appeared that the light of Christianity might be extinguished, churchmen prophesied that the end of the first millennium would signal the end of the world. When the fateful date had come and gone, not only was the world still in place, but many of the non-Christian invaders had been converted as well.

The millennium was a new dawn for western Europe. Classical architecture was rediscovered, a spirit of hope was revived, and that spirit was reflected in a flurry of church building. "It was as if the whole earth, having cast off its age by shaking itself, were clothing itself everywhere in a white robe of churches,"[3] wrote a monk, Raoul Glaber, in 1003. These churches, forerunners of the true medieval cathedrals, were called Romanesque, a term coined in 1818 to describe the architecture, which took classical Roman techniques in new directions.

Romanesque churches were different from those preceding them. The arch came into greater prominence. Indeed, early Romanesque naves became long continuous arches called tunnel or barrel vaults. Size was still important, and the barrel-vault churches had extremely thick walls. The heavy roofs exerted such tremendous pressure outward, as well as downward, that half-barrel vaults were built on each side to brace the walls.

Since barrel-vault churches needed every foot of solid wall possible in order to support the roof, windows were small and far between. The result was a very dim, subdued interior, but this matched the monastic spirit in which many churches were built. Unlike the medieval cathedrals to follow, these abbey churches were built for men and women retreating from everyday life. These gloomy buildings virtually shut out the outside world, enabling those who prayed there to look deep within themselves.

The nave of the Saint-Sernin in Toulouse, France, is comprised of long continuous arches called barrel vaults.

THE ROMANESQUE REQUIREMENT

The Romanesque style of building enabled cathedrals and monasteries alike to become larger. The great size was not needed for the monks who lived in the monasteries or for the people in the cathedral city. It was needed for the crowds of pilgrims who, once the Dark Ages ended and relative peace came to Europe, flocked to churches to worship at the site of relics. Art historian Louis Hourticq, quoted in *The Heritage of the Cathedral* by Sartell Prentice, describes the need for space, not only to hold crowds but also to enrich churches.

Once the Dark Ages ended, many pilgrims flocked to churches to worship relics.

The more famous sanctuaries attracted so many of the faithful that the aisles of churches had to be enlarged and ambulatories created; buildings were made more spacious to receive the crowds who were huddled together in the small churches of that earlier [basilica] style. The imposing architecture of [the cathedrals at] Vézelay and Autun, of S. Giles and Arles, is infinitely too vast for the requirements of an ordinary abbey church. It was intended to serve worshipers far beyond the parochial limits, those itinerant congregations who came to pray to the [Mary] Magdalen, to Lazarus, to S. Giles, to S. Trophîme. Offerings enriched sanctuaries; cures and miracles paid for costly churches, for their sculptures, for their goldsmith's work, their ivories, and their precious stuffs.

GROIN VAULTING

The early Middle Ages receded, and with them went the need for a fortress-church. Architects looked for ways to make churches less massive—to reduce the weight of the roof in order to reduce the thickness of the walls supporting it. Their answer was to abandon the barrel vault and to cross supporting arches diagonally over sections of the nave, thus forming a series of bays. The weight, instead of descending evenly on the walls, was transferred to pillars on each corner of the bay. Naturally, the outward pressure at the points where the arches met the pillars was enormous, so sections of wall—buttresses—were placed at right angles to the exterior walls, replacing the half-barrel vaults.

The technique of crossing arches at right angles produced what was called a groin vault, and these were used not only to span the nave but also in the aisles, replacing the old half-barrel vaults. Through the use of groin vaults, the pressure of the roof, instead of being spread over the entire wall, was concentrated where the diagonal arches met the pillars and was counteracted by buttresses. Portions of the wall freed from the stress of supporting the roof could be used for windows, and churches began to admit daylight as never before.

The problem with early groin vaults was that they worked well only for square bays. The right height for the arch was one-half the length it spanned. Anything less produced too much vertical pressure and invited collapse. Thus, a bay other than square would require arches of different heights—unsightly and difficult to build.

MEDIEVAL CATHEDRAL: GROIN VAULT

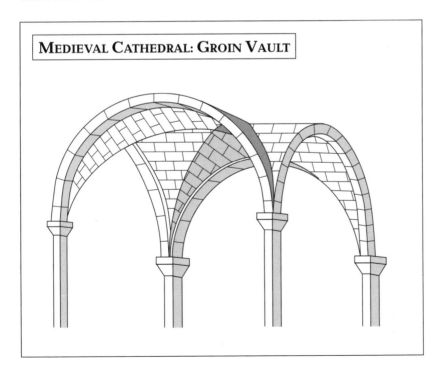

THE POINTED ARCH

The first solution was to have the arches rising from pillars of different heights. This produced arches the same height, but the uneven pillars were just as ugly as the uneven arches. The eventual answer, achieved during the late Romanesque period, was to make the arches pointed instead of rounded. The pointed arch did for the rounded arch what the rounded arch had done for the horizontal beam. The weight of the vault still went outward from the center, but the pressure was much more vertical, running down along the sides of the arch toward the ground.

The pointed arch was an improvement on the rounded arch because the pressure of the vault was directed down the sides of the arch toward the ground.

EXPRESSION OF CONTEMPT

The style in which medieval cathedrals were built was common in France, England, Germany, and Spain, but it never achieved popularity in Italy. Builders there, true to their Roman heritage, constructed their churches in the Romanesque style until the 1400s, when the Renaissance brought about a return to the classical architecture of Greece and Rome.

Consequently, the architects of Renaissance Italy had little good to say about the medieval style that they considered barbaric. Artist and critic Giorgio Vasari (1511–1574) linked it with one of the fierce tribes—the Goths—who had overrun the Roman Empire centuries before, describing it as, quoted in *High Gothic: The Age of Great Cathedrals* by Gunther Binding,

> something monstrous and barbaric, far removed from any harmony, and at best to be described as chaos and disorder. Many buildings of this type are now infecting the world. Their portals show relatively slim columns, which are also twisted in a screw-like fashion and are never formed strongly enough as to be able to carry a weight, no matter how small. This accursed style of design is accompanied by lots of confusing, small objects, which are to be found on all sides of the building, covering it almost completely, aligned one above the other and each decorated with a number of obelisks [towers], peaks and leaves. Such fragile-looking structures become even less stable when bundled together in this way, and they seem rather to be made of paper than of stone or marble. It was the Goths, too, who introduced pointed arches and filled the whole of Italy with their accursed designs.

Romanesque churches were beautiful, but in a solid, sober way. Architectural historian Sartell Prentice writes,

> [The Romanesque church] is no fragile or dainty thing; no wind of the north may blow it down; it stands, stout and strong, incarnating a spirit of endurance benefiting that anvil which has broken many a hammer. The dim lights

of the aisles, the shadows among the vaults, the unend-
ing twilight which gives a brighter radiance and a deeper
symbolism to the candles burning on the altar, all encom-
pass the worshipper with a sense of divine mysteries al-
ready half fulfilled.[4]

Another change was on the horizon. Romanesque architects
had absorbed the lessons of more than a thousand years of
church development. In turn, their struggles to master the construction of stone vaults had paved the way for later builders,
who would dispel the gloom and, by erecting soaring walls
seemingly more of glass than stone, produce the medieval
cathedral in its most pure form. These buildings, the glory of
western Europe, would be dismissed by those in other places at
other times. The Italian artist and critic Giorgio Vasari, writing
in the 1500s, compared them to one of the barbaric tribes that
had destroyed the grandeur of Rome. In doing so, he gave them
the name by which they are known today: Gothic.

THE GOTHIC VISION

The Gothic cathedral, the ultimate expression of the medieval spirit, was the result of a combination of factors that came together in western Europe in the mid-1100s. It was an era of relative peace. The church had withstood the threat of extinction during the early middle ages and had emerged as the dominant social and political force. Trade with the Middle East and Asia, the discovery of new sources of precious metals, and the rise of cities and a vibrant new merchant class provided the wealth that built the cathedrals.

These two elements came together at a single place at a single time and were forged together by a single person, Abbot Suger of Saint-Denis. Suger not only expressed the medieval spirit in his writings, but he also was in a position to turn that vision into a building that broke free from the massive gloominess of the Romanesque style. Since Suger's new church was dedicated to the patron saint of France and since Suger's patron was the king of France, it was no surprise that his vision—what would eventually be called Gothic—spread rapidly throughout Europe.

PEACE AND POLITICS

Modern historians have called the interval between 1000 and 1300 one of relative peace in western Europe. That opinion doubtless would have come as a surprise to the Saxons in England, who were crushed by William the Conqueror's invasion from Normandy in 1066, or to the

William the Conqueror routed the Saxons in England during his invasion from Normandy in 1066.

A statue of Otto the Great adorns Magdeburg Cathedral.

Spaniards, who were fighting desperately to drive the Moors back across the Straits of Gibraltar. Indeed, most people today would label these centuries ones of barbarism and almost continuous warfare. Compared to the Dark Ages that preceded them and the destruction spread by war and disease after them, it was a time of relative calm.

As a result of that calm, and other factors, it was also a time of prosperity. Agricultural methods, including crop rotation, improved the food supply. Even the weather cooperated. The climate of the 1100s and 1200s was far milder than in previous centuries. Starting in 1095, the Crusades—holy wars intended to "free" Palestine from Islamic rule—reestablished ties between the eastern Mediterranean and Europe. Previously unknown luxuries such as spices and fabrics were brought back by crusading knights, and the resulting demand fueled an increase in trade.

A MONEY ECONOMY

Europe began to develop a modern economy. The gold and silver mines that had furnished much of the wealth of the Roman Empire had played out in the 300s, but vast new deposits of silver were discovered near Rammelsberg in present-day Germany. The story goes that a horse in the hunting party of Emperor Otto the Great grew impatient during a halt and pawed the ground, disclosing a vein of silver. As a result of the new supply of precious metal, Europe evolved from an economy based on bartering to one based on money.

The money-based economy, increased trade, and generally peaceful conditions transformed the face of Europe. The manorial system—one based on landlords and tenant farming—declined at the same time as a new (for Europe, at least) and vibrant force rose: the cities. Merchants, instead of wandering the countryside in search of customers, established centers of trade, frequently at ports or at points where major roads crossed. Perhaps at first only a group of cottages, these centers grew into towns and then into cities. London increased from a population of 7,000 to 45,000 between 1100 and 1200. Paris went from 8,000 to 240,000 in the space of two hundred years. Religious zeal would furnish the spirit that built medieval cathedrals, but it would be the cities that furnished the wealth and the labor.

EUROPEAN POLITICS

Europe was not made up of nations in the modern sense. Italy and Spain did not exist as such but instead were patchworks of small kingdoms and principalities. Germany was similar, although the various segments, theoretically at least, made up the Holy Roman Empire with a single emperor. Just how unified the German states were depended on the strength of each emperor.

England and France had just begun to emerge as nations. England was unified, but the kings of England held large territories in France and were, under what was called the feudal system, subjects of the French kings—again, at least theoretically. In practice, the kings of England and France were heated rivals, and this rivalry eventually would erupt in a war that would hasten the end of the medieval spirit.

The kings of France were in an unusual position because much of their realm was ruled by the English and by powerful dukes who obeyed their king only when it suited them. Still, the French kings were the richest and most prestigious in Europe. Once confined mainly to the Île-de-France, an area immediately surrounding Paris, they had expanded their control over the agriculturally rich heartland of the country.

France was a center of culture, learning, and religion. The French court was the most splendid in Europe and set the fashion for all others. The university at Paris was unexcelled. And, even though Rome was still the spiritual capital, the intellectual spirit of the church came from the great monastic orders of France: the Cluniac, founded in 910 in the town of Cluny, and the Cistercian, founded in 1098 at Cîteaux.

The seal of the University of Paris, an institution that helped infuse the French churches with an intellectual spirit.

The abbots who governed the great monastic houses were answerable only to the pope, while most of the bishops and archbishops had ties to royal and ducal courts. And the popes, the strong ones at least, were the real rulers of Europe. People considered themselves citizens of Christendom, the kingdom of Christ on Earth, and the pope ruled in God's name. To defy the pope was to defy God, and even the strongest of medieval kings bowed to the papal will, however grudgingly.

THE DOMINANCE OF RELIGION

It is difficult for the modern mind to comprehend the extent to which religion dominated our medieval counterparts. To the Eu-

CAPTURING THE SPIRIT

Medieval cathedrals, to those who constructed them, were much more than mere buildings in which church services were conducted. They were intended to be reflections of humanity's understanding of God. As this understanding came to be defined in terms of a divine light, builders sought to bring this luminous aspect to their buildings. In 1859 a German art historian, Franz Kugler, quoted in *High Gothic: The Age of Great Cathedrals* by Gunther Binding, wrote that Gothic architecture represented

> a striving towards a light-filled sublimity and a unified articulation of space. Its builders were very much aware of the mystical effect of an architectural space which was needed for the inspiration of the spirit. . . . The mystical is woven into the totality of the Gothic building. . . . These spaces rise upwards, airily opening themselves up in the upper reaches to the fullness of light streaming in from outside, the roof seems to be held in swaying motion supported atop rising columns, without mass, like a miraculous vision. The secret of this effect which seems to flout the laws of nature lies in a structure put together with great feeling for its meaning. The entire building mass had broken down into a framework of individual parts, between which were placed only lighter infill sections to close it off from the outside.

ropeans of 1200, God governed the affairs of men not remotely but directly and immediately. They saw God's creation in everything, everywhere, and at all times. They believed that there was an order, a symmetry to creation, and that God was slowly revealing his ultimate purpose to humanity through everything he created. It followed that everything that people did was part of God's purpose and should reflect God's glory. This included what they built, particularly their churches.

The medieval church—whether a humble parish chapel or a magnificent cathedral—was the house of God, not in a figurative sense but very literally. Churches were held to be direct descendants of the ancient Jewish Temple of Solomon in Jerusalem. According to the Old Testament, Solomon's temple was built as an image of the Holy Tabernacle, or shelter, built by Moses according to God's explicit instructions to house the Ark of the Covenant, God's earthly dwelling place. Thus, when the people of the Middle Ages built churches, they sought to build them as images of God's heavenly city, according to God's will as they understood it to be.

The fortress-like exteriors of Romanesque churches such as the Languedoc in France (pictured) contrast with their ornate interiors.

The Gothic churches and cathedrals represented a change in the European interpretation of the heavenly city. To the Romanesque builder, the church should be strong, fortresslike on the outside while the inside should reflect heaven's inhabitants and splendors. Entering a Romanesque church was supposed to be like entering heaven. Paintings and statues depicted Jesus and the saints. Rich tapestries hung from the walls. Altars were covered with gold.

THE GOTHIC VIEW

The view that inspired Gothic churches was different, and the most influential proponent of the Gothic view was Bernard, abbot of the Cistercian monastery at Clairvaux in France from

Cistercian abbot Bernard believed that churches should reflect the symmetrical and well-ordered universe that God created.

1119 to 1153. Bernard was the foremost advocate of the Cistercian view that love of luxury had replaced love of God among the Cluniacs. He wrote that, to better be able to find God, monks should rid themselves of all distractions, move away from cities, and build monasteries in remote places—working, studying, and meditating. Through Bernard's influence, Cistercian churches began to reflect their simplicity of life, plain and unadorned.

Bernard still believed, however, that churches should reflect God's image, and Bernard's view was of God as creator of a symmetrical, well-ordered universe. His inspiration came from a passage in the biblical Book of Wisdom: "You [God] have ordered all things in measure and number and weight." This had been interpreted in the 400s by St. Augustine, who saw God as a skillful architect who expressed both beauty and divine purpose in geometrical perfection.

This coupling of divine perfection and geometric precision was to be one of the dominant themes in medieval cathedral architecture. Builders and churchmen reasoned that the more symmetrical and geometrically precise the building, the more it might lead those who worshiped there to a better understanding of God. Under Bernard's influence, Cistercian churches abandoned fanciful Romanesque ornamentation and relied on orderly, balanced geometric shapes. The more "harmonious" the shape, the more it expressed God's plan. A square with its four equal sides was preferable to an unbalanced rectangle. An equilateral triangle was superior to any other.

THE ROLE OF LIGHT

Light, however, was much more important than measurements in medieval cathedrals. Again, this was an interpretation of the nature of God, and again a single man, Suger of Saint-Denis, was primarily responsible. Just as important as Suger, however, was Saint-Denis itself.

Located just outside Paris on a loop of the Seine River, the abbey of Saint-Denis, part of the Benedictine order, was dedicated to the half-legendary figure sent from Rome to convert the French. He was beheaded in Paris, of which he was the first bishop, in 258 and supposedly carried his decapitated head to the area where the abbey stands. Over time the abbey became the holiest place in France. Generations of French kings are

CONDEMNATION OF LUXURY

The monastic movement founded by St. Benedict in the 600s called for monks to live in quiet simplicity, far from the temptation of worldly luxuries. In the 1000s and 1100s, however, the Cluniac order in France increasingly adorned its churches with rich tapestries and covered altars with gold. A Cistercian abbot, Bernard of Clairvaux, lashed out against such ostentation in a letter, "Apologia", to the Cluniacs. This excerpt is found in *The Cathedral Builders* by Jean Gimpel.

But I, as a monk, ask of my brother monks . . . "Tell me, ye poor (if indeed ye be poor) what doeth this gold in your sanctuary?" And indeed the bishops have an excuse, [being] unable to excite the devotion of carnal folk by spiritual things, do so by bodily adornments. But we [monks] who have now come forth from the people; we who have left all the precious and beautiful things of the world for Christ's sake; who have counted but dung, that we may win Christ, all things fair to see or soothing to hear, sweet to smell, delightful to taste, or pleasant to touch—in a word, all bodily delights—whose devotion, pray, do we monks intend to excite by these things? What profit, I say, do we expect therefrom? . . . To speak plainly, doth the root of all this lie in covetousness, which is idolatry; and do we seek not [spiritual] profit, but a gift? . . . The church is resplendent in her walls, beggarly in her poor; she clothes her stones in gold, and leaves her sons naked.

buried there. The oriflamme, a sacred banner under which French kings went into battle, was kept there. As a result of its religious significance and its association with royalty, anything done at Saint-Denis was bound to impact the rest of France.

Saint-Denis took on an even greater importance in 1124 when Abbot Suger conducted a rally on behalf of King Louis VI, his close friend and former schoolmate, who was threatened with an invasion. In the carefully planned ceremony, the king prayed before the relics of St. Denis, invoking the saint's help and promising rich donations to the abbey. His prayers finished, Louis rose and, standing before the altar, took up the oriflamme and appealed to the assembled nobles to join him in this holy cause. Many, even those who had been hostile to him, did so and the invasion was averted.

Louis made good on his promise of a donation, but it took many years of additional fund-raising before work began on the rebuilding of Saint-Denis in about 1137. During this time Suger formulated his vision for the new building, and at the center of that vision was an emphasis on light.

A statue on the facade of Notre Dame in Paris represents Saint Denis, a half-legendary figure who was decapitated during his attempt to convert the French to Christianity.

SUNLIGHT AND RELIGION

Throughout human history sunlight has been linked with the divine. Sun worship has been an integral part of religions all over the world. The Greek philosopher Plato called sunlight "not only the author of visibility in all visible things but generation and nourishment and growth."[5] The Bible describes Jesus as the "light of the world."

Suger, like his contemporary Bernard, took inspiration from St. Augustine, who wrote that human perception of God's will and purposes come from a divine light. An even greater influence on Suger, however, was Dionysius, a mysterious figure who was probably from Syria and lived during the 400s. Dionysius blended the teachings of Plato and the theme of Christian light into a theology that presented light as the most direct manifestation of God. As described by historian Otto von Simson, "The creation is the self-revelation of God. All creatures are 'lights' that by their existence bear testimony to the Divine Light and thereby enable the human intellect to perceive it."[6] In other words, the divine light shines on all things created by God, and all things, in turn, have an inner light that reflects God, however imperfectly.

Saint Augustine believed that the human perception of God's will and purposes came from a divine light.

Dionysius's theology appealed to Suger for many reasons. The French form of the name *Dionysius* is "Denis," and the French mistakenly believed that their patron saint and the Syrian writer were one and the same. So it was no wonder that Suger embraced his theology of light and employed it in the reconstruction of his abbey church.

"THE MOST SACRED WINDOWS"

Suger wanted the interior of the church to be surrounded, as much as possible, by light instead of by walls. To achieve this he combined architectural techniques that resulted in the first true Gothic church. Of its choir, he wrote that "the entire sanctuary

IN DEFENSE OF LUXURY

Abbot Suger, who built the first Gothic church at the abbey of Saint-Denis near Paris, was a contemporary of Abbot Bernard, who decried ostentation in churches. In reply to Bernard, Suger defended the richness with which he decorated his new church in this passage quoted in *The Cathedral Builders* by Jean Gimpel.

Let every man abound in his own sense. To me, I confess, one thing has always seemed pre-eminently fitting: that every costlier or costliest thing should serve, first and foremost, for the administration of the Holy Eucharist. *If golden pouring vessels, golden vials, golden little mortars used to serve, by the word of God or the command of the Prophet, to collect the* blood of goats or calves of the red heifer [in ancient Jewish ceremonies]; *how much more must golden vessels, precious stones, and whatever is most valued among all created things, be laid out, with continual reverence and full devotion, for the reception of the* blood of Christ! *Surely neither we nor our possessions suffice for this service. . . . The detractors also object that a saintly mind, a pure heart, a faithful intention ought to suffice for this sacred function; and we, too, explicitly and especially affirm that it is these that principally matter. But we profess that we must do homage also through the outward ornaments of sacred vessels, and to nothing in the world in an equal degree as to the service of the Holy Sacrifice, with all inner purity and with all outward splendor.*

The lavishly decorated interior of the abbey of Saint-Denis.

is thus pervaded by a wonderful and continuous light entering through the most sacred windows."[7]

No one knows how much of Saint-Denis was designed by Suger. He makes no mention of any master builder or architect in his description of the church and its construction. Architects, however, did not then exist in the modern sense. It was not unusual for the churchman or king who commissioned a building to communicate concepts to a master mason who executed them in stone. Therefore, it is safe to assume that Suger was the guiding genius behind this new type of building.

Certainly, Suger took great personal pride in what he had accomplished. He was pictured four times in his church, either in carving or in stained glass. He wrote thirteen inscriptions to himself and had them chiseled in stone or metal. One reflects his emphasis on light as the predominant feature of the church:

> Once the new apse is joined to the old façade
> The center of the sanctuary gleams in splendor.

Large stained glass windows dominate the altar of Saint-Denis, flooding it with light.

What has been splendidly united shines in splendor
And the magnificent work, inundated with a new light,
   shines.
It is I, Suger, who in my day enlarged this edifice,
Under my direction was it done.[8]

Suger had accomplished more than he realized. When the choir was dedicated in 1144, the magnificent ceremony was attended not only by the king and leading nobles but also by every archbishop and bishop in France. Awed by Suger's vision, they returned to their respective cathedrals, no doubt a bit envious and determined that they, too, should raise such a glorification to God. Economic, political, and religious events had conspired to produce the first Gothic church, and the age of the medieval cathedral had begun.

3

THE BUILDERS

Medieval cathedrals might have been intended as earthly reflections of God, but they were built by human beings. While the church was supposed to represent the heavenly city, an embodiment of divine light, it was nevertheless an earthly construction of stone, wood, and glass. The cathedral may have been divinely inspired, but it was the result of the labors of generations of workers—some renown, most obscure; some whose fame has endured through the centuries, most who have been forgotten.

Viewing medieval cathedrals from a modern perspective, it is easy to forget what a massive challenge they posed to those who built them. Their knowledge of architecture was primitive. Their tools were crude. Yet they were able to erect buildings that for centuries have inspired those who worship in them. In so doing, they set an example for later generations of builders, who owe much to those mostly nameless artisans. Later church architects might well have echoed Bernard of Chartres, who wrote in the 1100s that

> we are as dwarfs mounted on the shoulders of giants, so that although we perceive many more things than they, it is not because our vision is more piercing or our stature higher, but because we are carried and elevated higher thanks to their gigantic size.[9]

BISHOPS AND CANONS

Many of the key people in building medieval cathedrals never shaped a stone, never sawed a timber, never carved a statue. Yet without them, the cathedrals never would have been constructed. They were the churchmen who envisioned these grandiose plans, oversaw the myriad details and, perhaps most importantly, raised the money to pay for them.

Abbots and bishops frequently provided the initial inspiration to build the great churches and cathedrals but seldom were involved directly in construction. Abbot Suger of Saint-Denis and Bishop Evrard of Chartres in France were exceptions, taking active, day-to-day roles. Cathedrals, however, were usually built over decades. Bishops came and went. It was the chapter, with its dean and canons, who kept the project going.

The chapter originally was a group of priests who assisted the bishop, supervising the cathedral and the affairs of his diocese. The priests of the chapter were known as canons, and at their head was a dean. Once subservient to the bishop, by the Middle Ages the canons had grown largely independent. Unlike monks, they did not live communally but rather owned property and lived on revenues separate from those of the bishop.

The chapter normally controlled everything to do with the "fabric," the term used to describe the construction and maintenance of the cathedral. One of the canons was appointed *custos fabricae*, or "custodian of the fabric." During construction, the custodian supervised the hiring and payment of workers and the acquisition of materials.

Even before the design of a cathedral was completed, the task of assuring a supply of materials began. Massive amounts of timber were used, but timber was no problem because most of Europe was thickly forested. The critical element was stone. Ideally, stone would be used that was relatively easy to shape but that would resist harsh weather. Using stone from a single quarry was preferred, but this was very difficult since the deeper the quarry pits were dug, the harder it became to get rid of the water that seeped into them.

THE COST OF TRANSPORT

The location of the quarry was almost as important as the quality of the stone. Quarrying the stone was relatively cheap; transporting it was expensive. Transporting stone frequently cost three to four times as much as quarrying it. Heavy carts bogged down on the unpaved, muddy roads, and transportation by boat or barge was preferred. It was often much easier to move stone hundreds of miles over water than dozens of miles over land.

The chapter was in charge of raising the money to pay for everything from the most glorious stained glass to the wages of those who hauled debris from the site. The reason some cathedrals

took generations to build was not because of the difficulty of construction but
because work often had to be suspended
while the chapter raised more money.
When the normal revenues of the cathedral proved insufficient, the canons
sought new sources. "Their success,"
writes historian Jean Gimpel, "proved
them the equals of modern ministers of
finance with their unbalanced national
budgets."[10]

APPEALING FOR MONEY

The most direct way to raise money was
simply to ask for it. Periodic appeals from
pulpits exhorted rich and poor alike to
give what they could, and the canons
levied heavy taxes on themselves as
well. Many of the largest gifts were com-
memorated in stained glass windows:
The larger the gift, the more prominent
the window. The growing wealth of the

*Stained glass windows such as this one
depicting Joseph, Mary, and Jesus were
built with large donations.*

merchant class is reflected in the fact that in many cathedrals the
most prominent windows—those near the entrance and seen by
almost everyone who enters—were given by craft guilds while
those from the local nobility languish high up on the walls.

When normal appeals for donations proved insufficient, the
chapters might bring out the relics of their patron saints for display, charging pilgrims to view the leg bone of one saint or the
skull of another. When the local audience had been exhausted,
the canons frequently took the relics on tour. Records seem to
indicate that relics sometimes appeared to be in two places or
more at the same time. The canons might claim this to be a divine miracle, but the church had other ideas, and at a council in
1215, banned the showing of relics without permission.

An even more dubious method of raising money was the
sale of indulgences. Under this practice people were granted
forgiveness for their sins in exchange for donations: The more
serious the sin, the greater the donation. Eventually the traffick-
ing in indulgences became one of the prime factors leading to
the Protestant Reformation.

HIRING THE MASTER

Sometimes, especially with monasteries, the great churches of the Middle Ages were actually built by the religious community, whose members possessed the necessary skills. Most often, however, the chapter of a cathedral—those priests charged with its construction and maintenance—would hire an expert to supervise the building. These master builders were in great demand, and their reputations were known all over Europe. The hiring of a man to supervise the rebuilding of Canterbury Cathedral in England, which was damaged by a fire in 1174, was described by one of the canons and is found in *High Gothic: The Age of Great Cathedrals* by Gunther Binding.

William of Sens, a Frenchman, was for four years master builder of England's Canterbury Cathedral (pictured).

The brothers [canons of the chapter] had now sought advice as to how and in what measure of reason the burned church could be reconstructed, but they did not find it. . . . Thus skilled laborers were summoned from France and England, but even they were not in agreement in the advice they gave. . . . One of the labourers was a man from Sens [in France], William by name, a man active and ready, and as a workman most skilful in wood and stone. This man they took, and dismissed the others, because of his gift of lively invention and because of the good reputation of his work.

William of Sens worked for four years on Canterbury Cathedral until he was injured by a fall from the scaffolding. In the spring of 1179, when he realized that he would not recover to the extent that he could once more take an active part in the building, he gave up his post and returned to France.

MASTERS AND ARCHITECTS

During the early period of cathedral building, architects did not exist—at least not as the profession is understood today. The person in overall charge of both design and construction was most often a master mason who had acquired through experience a knowledge of geometry and building techniques. He was generally known as the *magister*, Latin for "master," a title that did not sit too well with scholars who thought it should be confined to those with an advanced academic degree.

Only in rare cases did the master builder draw plans for a cathedral. Instead, he carried only a general concept of size and style in his head. Only when construction actually began did he mark off with pegs and rope where walls, buttresses, and pillars were to be.

Master builders were paid much more—three to four times more—than other workers, even the most senior stonemasons. Their salaries were not only paid in money but also "in kind," which might consist of silver, firewood, food, and clothes. They were in great demand, and cities competed for their services.

The term *architect* began to be used later in the Middle Ages. As opposed to the master builders, the architects did no actual physical labor but were more like managers. Indeed, it seemed to Nicholas de Biard, a monk writing in the 1200s, as if they had risen too far above the rest of the workers:

> On these great buildings there is usually a main master who works only through the word, seldom or never laying his own hand to the work, and yet he receives a higher wage than the others. . . . Their only work is of the tongue, and they say, this is how you should do it. Yet they themselves do none of it.[11]

Architects like the one pictured here (third from left) managed the construction of cathedrals in the late Middle Ages.

Such was the prestige of master builders and architects that they frequently were buried in the cathedrals they had built in tombs similar to those of bishops and noblemen. One, Pierre de Montreuil, even gave himself an academic title higher than master, his epitaph reading, "Here lies Pierre de Montreuil, a perfect flower of good manners, in his life a doctor of stones. [O] that the King of Heaven will conduct [him] to the highest of poles!"[12]

THE MASONS

It was no coincidence that the vast majority of master builders and architects came from the ranks of the stonemasons. The masons were the most highly skilled and best paid of all of the cathedral workers, becoming fully qualified only after lengthy

Stonemasons, the most highly skilled and best-paid cathedral workers, are depicted on this stained glass window in Chartres Cathedral of Notre Dame.

apprenticeships. Specialists within the masons included the *cementarius*, who laid or set the stones; the *lathomus*, who carved them, the plasterers; and those who mixed the mortar that held the stones together. The mortarmen and plasterers were among the few groups that included women.

Stone carvers were further divided into "roughstone" masons— those who shaped the hard stones used for the walls and ceilings— and the "freestone" masons—who did the more delicate work in softer materials. The freestone masons eventually came to be called freemasons, and the communal lodges in which they lived were the origins of the modern Masonic Lodge social organization.

Each worker who shaped the harder stones used in basic construction had a distinctive symbol, or mason's mark, that was etched into each stone. These marks served two purposes. The first was to quantify the number of stones cut to determine how much the mason would be paid. The second was to identify each individual's work to the foreman who checked the stones for quality. As marks and their variations were handed down from master to pupil, father to son, they became symbols of pride, and masons inscribed their work much as an artist would sign a painting.

Quality control was by no means confined to the stones, however. Mortar and plaster had to meet rigid specifications, and the guilds, or workers' associations, enforced those specifications in order to protect the reputation of their professions. For instance, the *Book of Guilds* for the city of Paris spells out that

> no one may be a plasterer in Paris unless he pays 5 Parisian sous to the master [of the guild] who protects the profession for the king. When he has paid the five sous he must swear by the saints that he will put nothing in the plaster save lime and that he will give a good and true measure.[13]

QUARRYMEN

Those who worked with stone in the building of medieval cathedrals had both the best and the worst jobs. The mason was at the top of the scale; the quarryman was near the bottom. Enormous amounts of stone had to be dug out of the earth to build these monuments to heaven, and it was exhausting and often deadly work.

Most masons began their careers as quarrymen, digging deep into the pits, learning a feeling for the material. There were no explosives to blast the stone from its bed; instead, the quarrymen had to bore a series of holes into the rock and place wet timbers within the holes. When the timbers expanded, the stone cracked and huge blocks broke free.

The stone then had to be cut into blocks, laboriously hauled out of the pits, which frequently were filled with water, and taken to workshops to be shaped. Because of the high cost of transportation, it was necessary to dress, or shape, the stones into almost their final forms before they left the quarry. This was done by cutters in the workshop, which soon was filled with dust that entered the lungs of the workers and sent many to early graves.

Although masons, plasterers, and carpenters were skilled workers who moved from site to site, quarrymen were mostly local. Whereas about 85 percent of the quarrymen who labored at an English abbey between 1278 and 1281 were from the immediate area, only 5 to 10 percent of the masons were local. Indeed, the skilled artisans who worked on medieval cathedrals were unusual for the time because they moved from place to place while most people in medieval times lived their entire lives within a few miles of where they were born.

THE CARPENTERS

Although medieval cathedrals were essentially stone buildings and the masons were the most important workers, those masons could not have functioned without carpenters, known in medieval England as wrights. Wood was fundamental to the construction process, both as an aid to the masons and as part of the fabric itself.

The great stones that made up the cathedrals could never have been raised to such heights without the scaffolding erected by carpenters and the machinery they devised for lifting the enormous weights. Early in the medieval era, carpenters built wooden windlasses and capstans, which operated much like the devices that pulled ships' anchors from the water. When workers rotated the drum of a windlass, a rope on its circumference raised building materials to the proper level. Later, the carpenters devised a running wheel, a large wooden drum inside of which "winch boys" walked, turning the drum.

The most important task of the carpenters, however, was to provide a framework for the stones. Walls were no problem—stones could be placed atop one another and mortared into place with minimum difficulty. But what about the stones that made up the arches that spanned the ceiling? These relied on centerings—wooden frameworks on which the stones of the arches were cemented into place. Only after the mortar hardened could the wooden framework be removed.

The other principal part played by carpenters was in the construction of the roof. While the ceilings of cathedrals were made of stone, the roofs were made of wood, steeply pitched and covered with lead or tile sheeting so as to shed water and snow. To brace the roofs, carpenters used enormous beams sawed from entire tree trunks. Many of these beams still are in place.

Carpenters used the wooden windlass (pictured) to raise heavy building materials.

GLAZIERS, PLUMBERS, AND SMITHS

While the principal fabric of the medieval cathedrals was stone, glass was the material that gave them their chief characteristic. Glaziers, or glassmakers, were among the most highly skilled of cathedral workers, and many developments in glassmaking were made during the Middle Ages as a result of the growth of cathedrals.

At the start of the Middle Ages glass was expensive and rare. European glaziers lacked the skills to make large sheets of glass, so the large windows that were so much a part of Gothic cathedrals had to be made up of hundreds of small pieces arranged in designs. Late in the medieval period techniques improved to the point where larger panes of glass could be made, but with their use some of the charm of the older windows was lost.

Those who worked with lead were called plumbers, from the Latin word *plumbum*, meaning "lead." Unlike modern plumbers,

Founders were skilled workers who contributed to cathedral construction by casting bells.

however, their work was not chiefly the disposal of wastewater. Instead, they made the lead sheets that protected the wooden roof beams, the tubes for guttering, and the intricate frames to hold pieces of glass for windows.

Blacksmiths were also important to the construction of cathedrals, although they seldom worked on the actual building. Instead, they set up shops near the construction site. In these shops they made and repaired tools for the masons and carpenters and fashioned the iron strips and nails used to hold wooden beams together.

THE LABORERS

There were many other skilled workers who contributed to medieval cathedrals, including tapestry weavers, founders who cast bells and other items of brass, organ makers, locksmiths, and jewelers, but for every mason, carpenter, or other trained artisan, several persons were employed only in manual labor. Material that

THE CULT OF CARTS

The idealized notion has grown over the centuries that much of the work on medieval cathedrals was done by local citizens, rich and poor, who donated their labor as a gift to God. While historians now claim that volunteers played only small, insignificant, and occasional roles in cathedral building, such episodes have been recorded. One of the most fascinating was the Cult of the Carts in Chartres, France. An eyewitness, Abbot Haimon, described the phenomenon, as quoted in *The Gothic Cathedral* by Wim Swaan.

Who has seen or ever heard tell, in times past, that powerful princes of the world, that men brought up in honour and in wealth, that nobles, men and women, have bent their proud and haughty necks to the harness of carts, and that, like beasts of burden, they have dragged to the abode of Christ these waggons, loaded with wines, grain, oil, stone, wood and all that is necessary for the wants of life or for the construction of the Church. . . . They march in such silence that not a murmur is heard, and truly, if one did not see the thing with one's eyes, one might believe that among such a multitude there was hardly a person present. When they halt on the road, nothing is heard but the confessions of sins and suppliant prayer to God to obtain a pardon. At the voice of the priests who exhort their hearts to peace, they forget all hatred, discord is thrown far aside, debts are remitted, the unity of hearts is established.

today would be trucked to a construction site and lifted into place by gasoline-powered machinery had to be lifted, hauled, and forced into place by human muscle.

Some of the manual labor was done by apprentices, those learning any of the various crafts. Much, however, was done by local unskilled workers, glad for the opportunity to earn extra money. Some work was done without payment but as a gift to God. The most spectacular example of free labor occurred at Chartres in France with the Cult of the Carts. People of all ages and stations in life, even the men and women of noble families, harnessed themselves to wagons and dragged building materials and supplies to the construction site.

There are no records, however, of volunteer laborers actually working on the building itself. Far too much skill was needed. The role of pious volunteers, in fact, has been vastly exaggerated in romantic legend. Volunteers would have been highly resented by those from whom they took away much-needed employment. One story tells of a French nobleman, Renaud de Montauban, who joined a workshop as an act of piety, accepting only token payment. His fellow workers, worried that he would cause their wages to be lowered, beat him to death and threw his body into a river.

There can be little doubt, however, that most of the workers who built the medieval cathedrals had a sense that they were doing God's work, even if it was their livelihood. They took great pride in their work, but in the spirit of the age, they also found great spiritual comfort in contributing to a place of worship. In the south transept of the great cathedral of Notre Dame in Paris is an inscription, twenty-five feet long in letters carved eight inches high, reading, "Master Jehan de Chelles commenced this work for the glory for the Mother of Christ on the second of the Ides of the month of February 1258."[14] This inscription is one of the most spectacular examples of the combination of pride and piety that marked those who built medieval cathedrals.

4

Raising the Walls

Building a cathedral in the Middle Ages was not that much different from any major modern construction project. Certainly, tools were more primitive and medieval builders lacked such innovations as reinforced concrete, but it was still a matter of bringing workers, their tools, and materials together in a coordinated effort. The work was slow by modern standards, sometimes continuing over generations, but the cathedrals grew, stone upon stone, from the foundations deep under the earth to the pinnacle of the spire high above it.

One of the first problems the cathedral builders faced was the same one confronting any large project in the middle of a city: acquiring land. Medieval cathedrals were usually built on the site of older, often smaller structures. These smaller churches had, over the centuries, been surrounded by various kinds of structures, sometimes including other churches or monasteries. Before construction could begin, the cathedral chapter either had to buy up the needed property or to convince their neighbors to donate land. Sometimes property owners refused to move unless paid what they considered a fair price. As a result, many medieval cathedrals are narrow—not out of choice but because land to make them larger was too expensive.

Even before the land was acquired and the outline of the cathedral was marked out, the chapter and master builder began arranging for building materials, chiefly stone and wood. It took months to quarry stone, dress it to specifications, and transport it to the building site. Wood could usually be obtained more locally, but some pieces, such as the giant roofing beams, needed to be shaped and cured, or left to dry, for as long as a year before they could be put in place.

The Crypts

When the land had been cleared and the basic design of the master builder had been approved by the chapter and bishop,

Crypts such as this one at Saint-Denis held the tomb or relics of the patron saint along with the tombs of past bishops or abbots.

work actually began on the site. In cases where cathedrals replaced earlier churches, the layout was determined by the location of the crypt. The tradition of locating the altar directly over the tomb of the patron saint had expanded over the centuries, and most cathedrals and abbey churches had underground crypts that held not only the tomb or relics of the saint but also the tombs of past bishops or abbots.

Many of these crypts were hundreds of years old. Most were kept intact, but many had to be braced. Workers dug trenches along the outer walls of the crypts and built new retaining walls next to the older stones. In the rare cases where cathedrals were built on entirely new sites, bodies in the crypt were translated, or moved, to new crypts with great pomp and ceremony.

When the locations of the future walls had been determined, they were marked out with rope stretched between wooden pegs. To ensure perfect 90-degree right angles, builders used triangles whose sides were in the ratio of 3:4:5—the measurements established by the ancient Greek mathematician Pythagoras.

FOUNDATIONS

Once the walls were marked, workers began to dig trenches for the foundations. Very few cathedrals were built as a total unit. Instead, they were built in phases. The choir and apse were normally built first, and when these were completed, services were conducted during the time the rest of the cathedral was under construction. The transepts would be built next, followed by the nave and any attached buildings such as a baptistry, bell tower, or meeting place for the chapter.

For the first phase of construction, the choir and apse, three sets of foundations were required. The innermost foundations held the giant piers, or vertical support pillars, on which the walls of the choir rested. Next came the foundations of the lower

ON SCAFFOLDING

One of the more important but less glamorous aspects of cathedral building was the wooden scaffolding used by workers as walls grew higher. French architectural historian Eugéne Viollet-le-Duc discussed the vital yet usually overlooked role of scaffolding in his study of Gothic cathedrals. This excerpt is found in *The Construction of Gothic Cathedrals* by John Fitchen.

A well-made scaffolding is a feature of the builder's art which engages his best intelligence and his thorough supervision, for the real skill of the builder can be judged from the manner in which he places his scaffold. Well-designed scaffolding saves time for the workmen, gives them confidence, and obligates them to regularity, method, and care. If the scaffoldings are massive, if they employ wood in profusion, the workmen are well aware of it: they judge the chief's degree of practical knowledge from this provisional work, and they recognize any inclination of his from this abuse of means. On the other hand, if the masons are called to work on a daring scaffolding whose solidity, in spite of its apparent lightness, is convincingly proved and quickly recognized after a few days, they very readily appreciate these qualities and understand that what is required of them is care and precision in their work: "almost" will not be good enough.

walls that would surround the apse and run down the outside of the aisles on each side. Finally trenches were dug for the foundation of the buttresses necessary to brace the choir walls.

Ideally, these trenches would reach down to firm bedrock, on which the base of the walls would sit. Builders, however, seldom had the luxury of getting to choose an ideal site, usually building on the site of an existing church and dealing with whatever conditions they found.

Frequently, builders found moist, even marshy, soil, not bedrock. In such cases they normally drove a series of wooden piles, or huge poles, deep into the ground, and sawed the tops off to form a level surface. The tops then might be capped with iron heads and heavy planking overlaid to act as a footing for the wall. In rarer instances, such as at Notre Dame in Paris, built on an island, the entire site was ringed underground by a huge stone retaining wall designed to hold the soil in place.

THE FIRST STONE

When the trenches had been dug and the footings had been prepared, work on the foundation began, usually with a ceremony in which the bishop blessed the first stone to be lowered and put into place. Although work on the site may have been underway for months, it was at this moment that the building of the cathedral was said to have begun.

The masons who laid the stones of the foundation encountered the same problem as the quarrymen who had dug them from the earth—groundwater. Rainfall and underground streams are common in western Europe, and water was likely to seep into any large hole in the ground. Except in the driest part of the summer, leather buckets of water had to be lifted out of the trenches before stones could be lowered into them.

The moisture was more than an inconvenience. Scientists examining medieval mortar have concluded that it took far longer to dry than modern mortar with chemical additives. Work on the foundations had to proceed slow enough to give the mortar between the bottommost stones time to set before too many more layers were added.

The most solidly built cathedrals had foundations of stone going all the way to bedrock. Since stone was very expensive, however, some builders saved money by filling the trenches almost to ground level with small rocks and stones before starting to lay the larger shaped stones. Over the centuries these foundations tended to sink under the enormous weight of the walls.

THREE-STAGE WALLS

The walls, however, were nowhere near as massive as in the earlier Romanesque churches. The apse and choir were ringed by a wall that ascended in three levels. The lower level—the arcade—was solid stone only for a few feet near its top. On this solid part of the arcade rested a series of giant piers, or columns—eighty to one hundred feet high, with pointed arches in between. The arches provided passage from the choir into the apse and, on the other side of the transepts, from the nave into the side aisles.

The second level of the choir was the triforium, so called because it occupied much the same position as the old triforia galleries

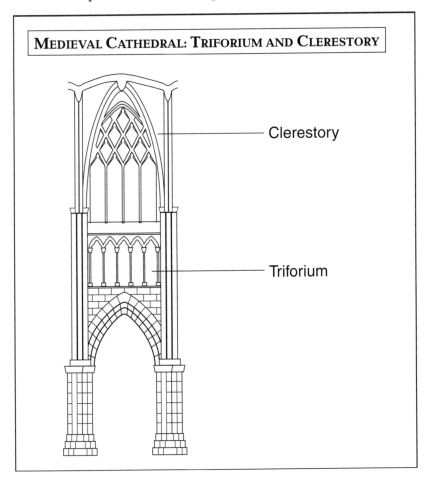

MEDIEVAL CATHEDRAL: TRIFORIUM AND CLERESTORY

Clerestory

Triforium

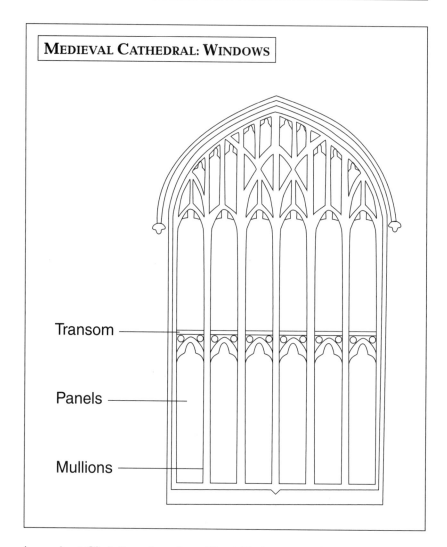

MEDIEVAL CATHEDRAL: WINDOWS

Transom

Panels

Mullions

in ancient Christian churches. The triforium was the least tall of the three levels—perhaps twenty feet—with two or sometimes three smaller arches between each pier instead of one large arch as in the arcade. In some cases the interiors of the triforia arches were filled with freestone and were covered with carved decorations. In others, the arches contained stained glass windows.

The third level, and the glory of the Gothic cathedral, was the clerestory, soaring sixty feet or more above the triforium. The walls were the ultimate expression of what Robert Grosseteste, bishop of Lincoln in the 1200s, called "the word of God, Light of the Father, that had passed through the body of the Virgin."[15] They were not walls as much as they were huge expanses of colored glass through which sunlight was filtered. The columns were narrower than in the gallery, and the areas in between were divided into tall windows by even narrower columns or by iron bars called mullions.

WORKING THE STONE

Work on the walls was highly organized. Stones had been transported to the building site by boat or barge if at all possible.

GALLERIES AND VICES

Medieval builders recognized the fact that, once a cathedral was completed, some route had to be provided for future workers to have access to the building's upper reaches, both to make inspections and effect repairs. The solution was to provide galleries, walkways located above the arcades, and sometimes between the triforium and clerestory. The galleries, which could be either interior or exterior, were described by architectural historian Eugéne Viollet-le-Duc, as quoted in *The Construction of Gothic Cathedrals* by John Fitchen.

Spiral staircases known as vices provided a pathway for workers.

> The galleries are always useful. In their great buildings the medieval architects established the means of easy circulation at different levels in order to provide surveillance of and maintenance to the building's fabric, to the roof coverings and the stained glass, without being obliged, as we are nowadays, to erect expensive and harmful scaffoldings, harmful by reason of the damage they cause to the carving and the delicate portions of the architecture.

Access to the galleries were by spiral stone staircases known as vices. These were purely functional rather than decoration, and they were usually tucked far into a wall or into a buttress, hidden behind obscure doors. Not only did the vices provide access for workers long after the cathedral's completion, but they also provided a pathway during construction for workers carrying lighter materials.

Roughstone masons at the quarry site had, according to the master builder's plan, shaped the stones into rough blocks. When they arrived at the building site, other masons finished the dressing, squaring the corners and smoothing the sides.

Oxcarts hauled the dressed stones to an area near the walls, where they were stacked neatly. From there, they were carried to the walls by laborers using a barrow. Barrows looked something like stretchers, having a flat surface with handles at each end. At some point during the Middle Ages a clever builder discovered a way to enable one laborer to do the work of two by attaching a wheel to one end of the barrow and inventing the wheelbarrow.

Elsewhere, other workers were busy making the mortar that would hold the stones together. They roasted chalk, limestone, or shells in a burner to extract quicklime. They then made the mortar by mixing quicklime, sand, and water in exact proportions, stirring them together in a large pit lined with clay. The finished mortar was then carried to the walls. Through experience the master builder would know just how much mortar should be made to supply the masons for the day's work so that none would be wasted.

Masons laid the finished stones atop one another in layers, with mortar in between. The mortar was applied with a triangular metal tool called a trowel, virtually the same as those used by modern bricklayers. Mortar was usually carried to the mason on a square board. The shape of the board and its name—mortarboard—was adopted by universities during the Middle Ages for the headwear still worn at graduations and other academic ceremonies.

Workers shown on this stained glass window use a barrow to transport stones to the cathedral wall.

Work could progress fairly rapidly where the walls were solid. The walls of medieval cathedrals, however, were filled with arches, and the stones forming the arches had no other stones on which to sit. To provide a frame, carpenters made falsework, or wooden outlines of the arches. When the falsework was fastened in place, the stones of the arch were mortared into place. Once the mortar dried, the

The trowel wielded by this modern bricklayer is almost identical to those used by medieval stonemasons.

falsework was removed. Falsework not only served to hold the stones in place but also ensured that the arches would be uniform since the same model was used for all similar arches.

CHECKING THE WORK

As the walls grew taller, the master mason frequently checked to make sure they were perfectly vertical. The slightest deviation from vertical at the base of the wall could result in the top being several feet from where it was supposed to be. Also, walls that leaned were much more likely to collapse. To check that a wall was perfectly vertical, the mason used a plumb rule, a board with a string and weight attached. When the board was placed against a wall, the string was supposed to hang perfectly straight along a previously drawn line.

The master mason had to take just as much care to ensure that each row of stones was level. A wooden triangle was placed on the row of stones. If the row was level, a weighted line hanging down from the apex of the triangle would strike the proper mark on the base of the triangle.

Buttresses connect exterior piers to cathedral walls, countering the outward thrust of the roof and ceiling.

Getting the stones to the mason was almost as difficult and intricate a job as ensuring that they were level and vertical. As the walls grew higher, the masons worked from scaffolds. While modern scaffolding has a lightweight metal framework, the medieval versions were made of wood. Since they were frequently taken apart and reerected in other places, no attempt was made to fasten the frame together with nails or plates. Instead, the poles were lashed together with rope and planks were placed across them to hold the workers and their materials.

BUTTRESSES

As the walls grew taller, so did the great piers alongside them. Formerly, buttresses had been short, thick walls at right angles to the main wall. In Gothic cathedrals, however, buttresses were archways of stone stretching from the exterior piers to the walls to hold them in place, countering the outward thrust of the roof and ceiling. These archways, soaring from piers to walls high above the ground, came to be known as flying buttresses.

Various devices were used to lift the stones onto the scaffolding. All of them involved the turning of a drum around which a rope was wound, lifting the load. One was a simple windlass, with either one or two men turning cranks attached to a small drum. Another was a capstan, with the workers walking around a drum, pushing on poles inserted into the center. The most innovative was a very large drum in which one or two workers, usually boys, would walk, much like hamsters in a wheel. As the drum revolved, it wound a rope that lifted the load. This device was used for very heavy stones and beams and was so heavy itself that it was normally kept on the ground with the rope looped over a pulley.

HOLLOW WALLS

Cathedral walls were thick at the base, but not as thick as they appeared to be. While castle walls were solid stone throughout, sometimes as much as fifteen feet thick, such massive walls were not needed for cathedrals, which were supposed to be places of worship rather than fortresses. Moreover, solid stone walls were expensive. So, to give the appearance of solid stone plus the width necessary to hold the weight of the higher portions of the wall, the lower levels were made up of two parallel courses of stone with the space between filled with small rocks and rubble. Sometimes rows of stone were laid from one portion of the wall to the other at intervals to lend support.

Another reason why the lower parts of the walls did not need to be solid stone was because the upper walls they had to support were not solid either. Indeed, the walls of the clerestory consisted mostly of windows. The spaces within the windows were filled with delicately carved stonework called tracery, so-called because the designs were traced on a floor to provide a life-size pattern for masons to follow. Highly skilled freestone masons carved the hundreds of stones that made up the pattern, laying them out on the floor of the tracing house. Later, they would be lifted into the arches and mortared into place, reinforced with iron bars.

Tracery was not confined to windows, however. Many of the finely detailed carvings that went above doorways were first laid out on the tracing room floor. While most cathedral statues

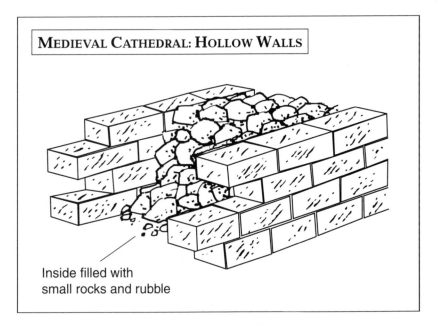

MEDIEVAL CATHEDRAL: HOLLOW WALLS

Inside filled with
small rocks and rubble

were carved separately and were later moved into niches in the walls, some were carved out of large blocks of stone that became part of the walls themselves.

A LONG PROCESS

Cathedral walls took several years to build at best. The slow-drying medieval mortar was even slower when exposed to wet

ONE YEAR AT A TIME

Cathedral building was, at its best, slow work. Transportation of materials was slow, and tools were primitive by modern standards. A monk, Gervase, wrote about the history of the building of Canterbury Cathedral in England. This excerpt is found in *High Gothic: The Great Cathedrals* by Gunther Binding.

And now he [master builder William of Sens] addressed himself to procuring stone from overseas. He constructed ingenious machines for loading and unloading ships and for drawing cement and stones. He delivered moulds for shaping the stones to the sculptors who were assembled, and diligently prepared other things of the same kind. The choir [of the former church] thus condemned to destruction was pulled down, and nothing else was done in this year [1174–1175]. . . . In the following year . . . he erected four pillars, that is, two on each side, and after winter two more were placed, so that on each side were three in order, upon which and upon the exterior wall of the aisles he framed seemly arches and a vault. . . . In the third year he added two more pillars on each side, and decorated the two outer ones all around with marble columns, and because this is the point at which the choir and the arms of the transept are to come together, he fashioned these as the main pillars. . . . In the summer of 1178 he erected ten pillars starting at the transept, five on each side. . . . Also, before the winter two [more] vaults were constructed on both sides, but the increasingly heavy rainfall did not permit more to be done.

weather. Work on the walls had to be halted in winter because water from rain or snow would penetrate the mortar and then freeze, causing the mortar to crumble. During this time, the partially completed walls were covered with a mixture of straw and animal dung for protection. Masons spent most of the winter months either at home with their families or with other masons in their lodge.

With the completion of the walls, the first phase of the building of the medieval cathedral was completed. The walls towered high above the ground, the windows empty. It was an impressive sight but not yet a functional building. Up until now the work had been relatively uncomplicated. Bridging the walls with a roof and a ceiling was a far more formidable task.

5

ROOF AND CEILING

The roofs and ceilings of medieval cathedrals served much the same functions as their modern counterparts. The ceiling provided a top to the interior space, and the roof protected the fabric of the ceiling from rain or snow. The covering of a cathedral, however, had significance that went far beyond function. The roof had to match the grandeur of the walls and windows, continuing the procession from level to level until culminating in towers and spires symbolic of fingers pointing to heaven. The same symbolism held true inside, with worshipers looking up past the light streaming through stained glass to the ceiling high above as if raising their eyes to God.

In addition to its symbolism, the cathedral ceiling was a test of the architect's skill. Tons of stone went into the arches, ribs, and areas in between, and the entire structure had to span the nave without supporting piers. Vaulting, the process of constructing the ceiling, was the most difficult of all of the processes of cathedral construction.

Before work could begin on the vaulting, there had to be a roof. Before a roof could be built, the walls needed to be buttressed. The buttress piers occasionally were built against the main wall, but most often they were a few yards to one side, with an arched walkway in between. In some cases sets of piers were built one outside the other. The buttresses themselves were arches of stone extending from the buttress

The spires of churches such as Notre Dame in Strasbourg, France (pictured) represent fingers pointing to heaven.

piers to the wall at points where the main piers outlining the nave and choir stood. These arches, "flying" from pier to wall, took on the outward thrust of the roof and ceiling, transferring it to the pier and down to the ground.

As cathedrals became larger and the thrust heavier, the buttress piers needed additional weight. This was provided by pinnacles, stone towers, and spires rising from the piers. The pinnacles were often decorated with stone projections called finials. Pinnacles and their finials often reflected the shape of the main spire of the church. Over the centuries, what had started out to be purely functional became an art form in its own right.

Pinnacles reflected the shape of the main spire of the church and were often decorated with stone projections called finials.

Centerings

Construction of the arches between piers and walls was accomplished much the same way as with the arches within the walls, only on a far larger scale. Instead of light falsework, carpenters built huge wooden frames the same size as the arches. On these large falsework frames, called centerings, the stones of the arches were laid. The very widths they needed to span made centerings large and heavy, and they needed to be strong to support the weight of the stonework. Yet builders did not want to make them too cumbersome since they had to be raised to great heights, moved into place, then taken down and reused. It is no wonder, as architecture professor John Fitchen writes, that

centering was certainly the most demanding erectional problem encountered by the medieval builders. When its inherent difficulties are considered along with the builders' evident determination to rationalize and reduce the amount of material used for the falsework structure, it is inescapably clear that the design and technique of placing centerings became a major preoccupation of the

FROM TRUNK TO TRUSS

Modern sawmills, with their electric-powered, high-speed equipment, can reduce a tree trunk to a smooth-sided wooden beam in just a few minutes. Medieval builders were not so fortunate, though. It did not take exceptional skill to make the giant roof beams that went into cathedrals, but it took a lot of muscle.

One reason fashioning a beam was such hard work was that only the hardest, strongest woods were used. Oak was a favorite, and it took a thick, tall, straight trunk to make the beams that would span the nave.

After the bark and limbs were stripped away, the trunk was secured over a large pit. Here, it was sawed into rough shape by men using a two-handled saw, one man standing in the pit under the trunk and the other above.

When the beam had been roughed out it was trimmed into a square shape with an adze, an axelike tool with a chisel head mounted at a right angle to the handle. More smoothing was done with a spokeshave, a steel blade with a handle on each end. Workers would grasp a handle with each hand and pull the blade toward them, planing the wood.

Once finished, the beams had to sit for months, stacked so as to permit air to circulate around them, before they were dry enough, or cured, and could be used. Carpenters took extraordinary care with beams, making them as smooth and even as possible. In some medieval cathedrals it is difficult to tell which roof beams are original and which are replacements cut with modern equipment.

architects, exacting from them the utmost in resourcefulness, ingenuity, and practical experience.[16]

Once the centerings were in place, wedge-shaped stones, known as voussoirs, were laid atop them and mortared together. When the flying buttresses were finished, which was a long time because all sides of the slow-drying mortar were exposed to the weather, work could begin on the roof.

ROOF TRUSSES

The frame of the roof consisted of a series of huge triangular trusses. The beams were made from tree trunks patiently sawed and planed into shape. The beams would have been shaped many months in advance of when they were needed to give the wood time to dry and season.

Much like tracery, the roof trusses were assembled on the ground and then taken apart. Lifting each individual beam was challenge enough; lifting the entire truss was beyond the ability of the machinery of the time. Using pulleys attached to scaffolding, the largest of the beams were lifted to the tops of the walls and put into place. These were the tiebeams, which formed the base of the triangle and stretched across the nave. Since the outward thrust of the weight of the roof would be greatest on the trusses, the tiebeams were placed at points on the wall opposite the flying buttresses.

Once the tiebeams were in place, the carpenters laid planking across them to form a temporary floor. This floor could be used as a work space and as a platform on which to place a windlass to hoist the other beams from the ground. The beams were held together by the mortise-tenon method rather than with nails. Mortises, or notches, were cut into the wood, into which tenons, or tongues, on corresponding beams would fit. Once the tenons and mortises were fitted, carpenters hammered wooden pegs into the joints to make them secure. Once joined, the beams were coated with tar to help them resist rotting.

When the trusses were in place, smaller rafter beams, called battens, were placed lengthwise across the sides of the triangles along the body of the choir and nave. Onto the battens was fastened whatever material had been selected for the permanent roof cover. If money was a problem, wooden shingles might be used until the chapter could afford something better, but wooden roofs were vulnerable to fire. Tiles or slates were better, but they tended to break.

LEAD ROOFING

Up to the Gothic era, the most popular roofing material had been lead, which was soft enough to be rolled by the plumbers into long, thin sheets that were laid vertically across the battens and interlocked to prevent leakage. Lead had the advantage of being fire-, rot- and waterproof. Cost and weight were the drawbacks. Most Gothic cathedral roofs, however, were steeply pitched—up to sixty-five degrees compared to forty-five degrees or less in Romanesque churches. Lead roofs could not be as steeply pitched as others because the sheets were so heavy that, if placed at a steep enough angle, they would roll down the sides of the roof like a carpet. Consequently builders had to use tile or slate for many medieval cathedral roofs.

Roofs were as steep as possible for two reasons. One was appearance; a tall, tapering roof looked much better atop the steep walls than one that was short and squat. The second reason was functional. Leaks most often occur when water stands on a roof. On a steep roof, water rushes off before it has a chance to find a crevice.

Builders, however, could not let rain simply pour off the roof in all directions, perhaps onto people below. They also did not want water running down the sides of the walls and discoloring the stonework. To control the flow, they used a system of gutters and channels to funnel the water. The guttering was made of lead, again because it was easy to mold. Water ran through the gutters, down channels in the flying buttresses, and out through spouts that directed it away from the walls.

Tall, tapering roofs were chosen for medieval cathedrals because they are aesthetically pleasing and help prevent leaks.

Intricately and imaginatively carved structures called gargoyles functioned as rain spouts for medieval cathedrals.

GARGOYLES

Even an object as ordinary and functional as a rain spout could be made into a work of art by medieval craftspeople. Simple stone spouts eventually gave way to intricately carved structures called gargoyles, from the old French word for "gargle." Masons used considerable skill and imagination in carving gargoyles into fanciful shapes, including dragons, devils, and mythical monsters. Water rushed through the elongated bodies of the gargoyles and out of their mouths, giving the impression from below that the gargoyles were spitting.

Gargoyles were typical of the type of care that medieval workers took with every part of a cathedral. Even though they were high above the ground, almost indistinguishable from below, they were carved with the same skill and thoroughness as if they were to be on view inside the front door.

SPIRES AND TOWERS

Spires and towers were the crowning glory of medieval cathedrals. Generally speaking, towers seem to have been preferred in

Spires, symbolic of striving toward heaven, were points of pride with citizens and religious figures from the surrounding area.

England and spires elsewhere in Europe, although examples of both styles are found everywhere. Both had the original purposes of holding the great bells used to call the faithful to services and of furnishing a point from which to watch for danger in wartime. In the later Middle Ages they also housed clocks.

The number and location of the spires and towers varied. Some cathedrals had only one. In that case, it usually was built directly above the crossing of the nave and transepts. Other churches featured two towers or spires, one on either corner to the sides of the main doors. Still others had three or more. Some had combinations, such as spires to the side of the front doors and a tower above the crossing.

Spires evolved from modest pointed roofs to keep water from collecting on top of bell towers in the days when most construction was of wood. Over the centuries this roof grew more pointed and more ornate until, as with so many other elements of the medieval cathedral, it became mostly decorative.

Spires, like the soaring walls and pointed roofs, were symbolic of a striving toward heaven. They were also points of pride with the bishop, the canons of the chapter, and the citizens of the surrounding area. Just as the churches of modern cities may have a rivalry as to which has the highest steeple, so cathedrals competed to see which spire could be made the tallest. The spire of Salisbury Cathedral in England soars 404 feet above the ground, but the tallest of all medieval cathedral spires was that of Strasbourg in Germany, towering 490 feet or the equivalent of a forty-five-story building. Indeed, Strasbourg Cathedral was the tallest building in Europe until the 1,043-foot Eiffel Tower was built in Paris in 1889.

Spires were made of wood and were covered with thin sheets of lead nailed into place. The lead covering presented two problems. First, it made the spires so heavy that they sometimes

OPENWORK

The Gothic style of cathedral building advanced more slowly in Germany than it did in most European countries. However, when German builders began to design in the manner of their French counterparts, they took churches—literally—to new heights. The technique they used, called openwork, consisted of a much greater use of open space, almost like latticework.

Using openwork, it became possible for cathedral spires to grow taller than ever before. The technique was begun by master builder Erwin von Steinbach at Strasbourg. The facade he began in 1274, and which was not finished until about 1350, used massive amounts of tracery to produce an effect almost like lace. Indeed, some writers refer to openwork as "stringing."

The technique was later extended to the spire. It became fashionable in Germany to take advantage of the comparative lightness of openwork to build one giant spire instead of multiple towers and spires. Jean Gerlach, who succeeded von Steinbach at Strasbourg, planned twin spires 380 feet high, but his plans came to an end when Europe was ravaged by plague. When work was resumed, a

The 590-foot spire at Ulm Minster.

new design resulted in the giant 490-foot spire, called by historian Ann Mitchell in her book *Cathedrals of Europe* "a structure as daring and presumptuous as the original Tower of Babel."

The tallest spire on a medieval cathedral was not built in the Middle Ages. In the 1890s the citizens of Ulm in Germany decided to remodel their cathedral spire to the original design, which had never been undertaken. When finished, the spire at Ulm Minster reached 590 feet from the street below.

collapsed under their own weight. Second, the metal attracted lightning, which caused many fires. Eventually, all of the lead spire coverings were replaced with slate.

Towers were constructed of stone, which presented an even greater weight problem. Although they appeared solid from the outside, the towers were hollow except for the spiral staircases necessary to get to the top. In many cathedrals the bottom of the tower was open, allowing those below to see up to the top, which was frequently covered with elaborate carvings or paintings.

Still, towers were extremely heavy, and the piers on which they rested had to be considerably larger than others. Another problem came when spires were occasionally replaced by towers. Special buttressing had to be used for the piers, and sometimes extra arches had to be built to help support the weight. Even then, towers were often too heavy for the foundations and would sink to one side, creating a danger of collapse.

VAULTING

Once the protective cover of the roof was in place, work on the interior ceiling, the vaulting, could go forward. Vaulting was for the masons what centering was for the carpenters—the most challenging portion of the medieval cathedral. The question was one of how to span a wide area with a stone ceiling while relying on a minimum of piers. The two key elements in the answer were the pointed arch and the rib. These two elements, along with the flying buttress, are the hallmarks of Gothic cathedrals.

The space spanned by a round arch is limited to twice the height of the arch. If the arch is required to extend over a wider area, it may collapse under its own weight. The stones of a pointed arch, however, rest more atop one another. The weight is therefore distributed downward along each side of the arch until it meets a supporting pier.

It would have been impossible, however, to construct a ceiling consisting of a continuous series of transverse ribs—those stretching across the nave and choir. It would have been far too heavy and, in addition, would have been very plain in appearance from below. The solution was to stretch stone ribs diagonally between piers, thus dividing the ceiling above each bay of the cathedral into four quadrants. The space between the ribs then could be filled with a lighter material—bricks or small stones—known as the webbing.

VAULT CENTERING

Centering was just as important for the vaulted ceiling as for the flying buttresses. The wall ribs—those within the walls—and the transverse ribs were the first to be built. A few voussoirs were put into place on the main piers that eventually would support the arch. These were slightly longer than those that would be above them, and the extra length provided a ledge on which the centerings would sit. When the centerings were in place, more voussoirs were laid atop them until the arches were complete.

When the transverse arches were in place, larger diagonal centerings were placed between the corners of the bays and the process was repeated. The last stone to be put in place was the central keystone in the center where all of the diagonal ribs met. The keystone

Medieval cathedral vaults were constructed by stretching stone ribs diagonally between piers, thus dividing the ceiling into four quadrants.

was much larger and heavier than the voussoirs. Its purpose was not only to join the ribs together but also to put weight on the diagonal arches, which otherwise would tend to rise under the pressure exerted by the flying buttresses.

As usual, the masons took every opportunity to turn a functional item into a decoration. The underside of the keystone was elaborately carved, usually into floral designs, shields, or even biblical scenes. These carvings were traditional, copying the wooden bosses used to cover the intersection of beams in earlier wooden ceilings.

DECENTERING

When the ribs were completed, the centerings were removed for reuse in the next bay. This was not as easy as it may sound. The centerings did not rest flat on the protruding voussoirs. If they had, they never would have been able to be taken down without tearing them completely apart. Instead, wooden wedges

RIBS WITHOUT CENTERING

As the skill of medieval builders increased, it became possible for them to build the ribs of a vaulted ceiling using only a light falsework for support instead of heavy centering. This was made possible by two developments. Masons grew more adept at cutting stones that fit together more precisely than before, and the makers of mortar found ways to make their product dry more quickly.

In 1831 one M. de Lassaux, architect to the king of Prussia, wrote a journal article in which he described the advantages of such construction. This excerpt is found in *The Construction of Gothic Cathedrals* by John Fitchen.

> The advantage of this kind of vaulting without centering consists, not only in the very considerable savings of boarding, and of the greatest part of the centering arches, but it gives also a firmer vault; since the settling takes place gradually before the usual closing of the vault: indeed, the author almost doubts whether such thin vaults could be constructed at all upon a boarded centering. Except this is supported by scaffolding to an immoderate degree, the mere motion of the labourers, in the course of the vaulting, must cause a perpetual shaking, and, consequently, separations in the vault after it is begun; and even when the vault is brought to its closing, and it is wished to loosen the centering, which is so extremely advantageous for the uniform closing of all vaults, the inevitable consequence is bellying and cracking. If, on the other hand, we wish to leave the centering standing till the complete drying of the vault, the wasting of the mortar would cause all the joints to open and crack. But the network formed by the mortar in all the joints, gives to a thin vault of heavy stone a peculiar strength.

were put between the centerings and the voussoirs. The wedges could be adjusted to make the centerings level. Moreover, when the arches were completed, the wedges could be removed to free the centering from the arches. Workers then passed rope slings under the centerings and the entire framework was pivoted away from the voussoirs and was lowered to the ground.

The ribs provided the framework for the bulk of the ceiling, which was made up of webbing far thinner than the voussoirs. When the ribs were firmly in place, masons placed lightweight curved boards, called lagging, across the intersection of the transverse and diagonal members. They then laid the webbing in rows, much like in a wall except that each course was longer as the space between the ribs lengthened.

Sometimes, particularly in English cathedrals, the vaulting was then covered with a layer of concrete almost as thick as the webbing. This was intended to make the vaulting more rigid, but frequently it caused more problems than it solved. First, it added a significant amount of weight to the ceiling. Second, the cement reacted differently to temperature than the mortar between the webbing and arches. The difference in expansion and contraction caused cracks in the ceiling. Eventually, most concrete coverings were chipped away.

THE ROLE OF RIBBING

Experts disagree about the importance of the ribs in medieval cathedrals. Some say that only the transverse ribs were needed and that webbing could have been placed between them in any pattern without additional support. Others say that the diagonal ribs were actually more important than the transverse in carrying the weight and maintaining the shape of the webbing.

What is certain is that builders came to appreciate the aesthetic aspects of ribbing. The basic ribbed vault was either quadripartite—two wall ribs, two transverse ribs, and two diagonal ribs dividing the bay into four parts—or sexpartite, with an extra transverse rib dividing the bay into six parts. As the Gothic cathedrals gave way to more elaborate structures in the late Middle Ages, ceilings became covered with patterns of ribs

In the late Middle Ages, decoratively ribbed vaults such as this fan vault in the Canterbury Cathedral in England became popular.

that were purely decorative. The most elaborate form was the fan vaulting popular in England.

Once the roof, towers, spires, and vaulted ceiling had been completed, the heavy work of constructing the medieval cathedral was substantially finished. The building, however, was by no means completed. It was essentially a shell—a beautiful shell—that still needed the decorative touches that would bring it to completion.

6

THE WORD MADE FLESH

As magnificent as the shells of medieval cathedrals were, with their towering walls, vaulted ceilings, flying buttresses, and sharply pitched roofs, they were not yet the earthly reflections of heaven's glory that their builders sought. They were magnificent, yes, but in a cold, hard way. They needed the dazzling color of glass, the gleam of gold, the majesty of statuary, and the gloss of intricately carved wood to make them complete.

The statues that abounded both inside and outside the cathedrals and the pictures displayed in thousands of pieces of glass were much more than mere decoration. They brought the holy scriptures to life before the gaze of worshipers, the vast majority of whom could not read. Adam and Eve, the Last Supper, the Crucifixion, the Last Judgment—they were all represented. No wonder the carvings and stained glass windows of medieval cathedrals have been called "the Bible of the poor." The French poet François Villon wrote in the 1400s how his elderly mother might feel on entering a highly decorated church:

> I am a woman, poor and old,
> Quite ignorant, I cannot read.
> They showed me, in my village church
> A painted Paradise with harps
> And Hell where the damned souls
> are boiled.
> One gives me joy, the other frightens
> me.[17]

A statue of Eve decorates the top of a balustrade at Notre Dame in Paris.

SYMBOLISM

There was nothing random about the plan for decorating a cathedral. Everything had a purpose and a meaning. Symbolism could be found everywhere. If a bay or a screen had twelve windows, it had been planned to represent Jesus' twelve disciples. Many baptistries, the chambers in which baptisms were performed, were octagonal, representing the six days of Creation, the day of rest, and one additional day on which to start the new life symbolized by the baptism. Other cathedrals had five steps ascending to the altar in memory of the five wounds suffered by Jesus at his crucifixion.

THE IMPORTANCE OF SYMBOLISM

Very little in a medieval cathedral was planned from a purely architectural standpoint. The appearance of the various components was important, certainly, but just as important was what it symbolized. Virtually everything was symbolic, including the number of pillars, the number and shape of windows, and the number of steps leading to the altar. Abbot Suger of Saint-Denis in France, in writing about the consecration of his church, talked about the importance of symbolism. This excerpt is found in *High Gothic: The Great Cathedrals* by Gunther Binding.

> In the middle [of the nave] 12 columns, which represent the 12 Apostles, in the second row again as many columns in the aisles, representing the number of the prophets, all lifted the building up high, like the Apostle building in a spiritual sense who says: You are now not guests and strangers, but walk with the Saints and are members of the House of God, built on the foundation of the Apostles and prophets, with Jesus Christ himself as its most excellent cornerstone, linking the two walls in which the whole building, both spiritually and physically, grows to become one holy temple in the Lord. The higher and the more befitting we endeavor within it to build in the physical sense, the more we will be taught that we, through our own efforts, are built up spiritually into a house of God in the Holy Spirit.

In later centuries, the workers who executed these things of beauty would be called artists and would be famous throughout the land as kings vied for their services. Those who created the magnificent statues and windows of the medieval cathedrals, however, were considered artisans rather than artists. They were highly skilled and were well paid, but the names of only a very few have come down through the centuries. As historian Jean Gimpel writes,

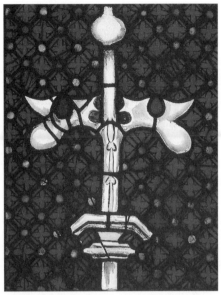

Stained glass became a major element of cathedral design in the Middle Ages.

> The truth is that for the great majority of men in the Middle Ages there was between a good *work* and a *masterpiece* only a difference of degree, not a difference of kind. The idea that there is an unbridgeable gulf between a worker and an artist (in the modern sense) did not really occur until the Renaissance, when it was expressed by intellectuals who judged, classified, and evaluated manual labor which was very foreign to them.[18]

STAINED GLASS

The glory of every medieval cathedral was its stained glass, although the term stained is often inaccurate. Rather than being stained, with colors applied to the surface, the glass of most early churches was colored throughout as part of the manufacturing process. Some early Christian churches had stained glass, probably in imitation of the mosaic tile patterns so popular among the ancient Greeks and Romans.

Stained glass as a major element of design, however, did not come into its own until the Middle Ages. The windows of earlier churches simply were too small. Even though perhaps filled with stained glass, they lacked the space for intricate designs or portrayals and did not occupy enough wall space to be a major decorative factor. However, with the Gothic emphasis on large expanses of windows as passageways for divine light, the glaziers, or glassmakers, found their places among the most honored artisans.

THE BEAUTY OF GLASS

To the bishops and monks who planned medieval cathedrals, God's perfection was reflected in earthly beauty, and one of the chief manifestations of beauty was light. When Gothic architecture made it possible to pierce the walls of churches with large windows, builders employed the light to create an aura of beauty by filling windows with stained glass.

Gunther Binding, in his book *High Gothic: The Great Cathedrals*, quotes Robert Grosseteste, bishop of Lincoln in England, as calling light

> beautiful in itself, because its nature is simple and at the same time contains all within it. For this reason it is to a high degree uniform and extremely harmoniously proportioned throughout its uniformity. Beauty is a harmony of proportion.

> And a monk, Durandus of Mende, also quoted in Binding, compared the windows of Strasbourg Cathedral to "holy scriptures, which hold off wind and rain, but which admit the light of the true sun, namely God, into the church, in other words into the hearts of the believers, and which bring enlightenment to those within."

As with many other parts of a cathedral, the glass windows were laid out on the tracing room floor and were lifted into place only when finished. The glazier first made a wooden panel exactly the size of the window to be filled. The panel was then covered with a thin layer of paste made with moistened chalk. The glazier then sketched out the design, indicating with letters or numbers the color for each of the hundreds of pieces.

The earliest material was called pot-metal glass. Washed sand, lime, and potash were combined in a metal pot and were heated to a high temperature. When the glass was molten, minerals were added that, over many years, had been shown to yield the best colors—cobalt for blue, nickel for red, selenium for yellow, copper for green. A glass blower would scoop up a blob of the molten glass on the end of a long pipe and blow the glass into a bubble. As the glass cooled, the blower cut off the end of the bubble and, by spinning the pipe quickly, was able to make the rest of the bubble flatten out into a circle. Another method was to cut the end off of the bubble and roll the remainder into a cylindrical shape that, while still very hot, could be cut and flattened.

FLASHING

Later, glaziers discovered the stained glass technique known as flashing. The blower would dip the pipe first into one color, then into a second, coating one color on another to achieve a third color. Red and blue glass was flashed to render purple, blue and yellow to yield green, and so on. Flashing began to be widely used in the late 1300s and is responsible for the most brilliantly colored cathedral windows.

When the colored glass had cooled and hardened, the glazier cut it into shapes, called quarries, needed to match a pattern. Diamond-tipped glass cutters would not be invented until the 1500s, so the medieval glazier had to use a grozing iron—a tool something like a metal pencil. First, the shape of the quarry was sketched out on the sheet of glass. Then, the glazier heated the pointed end of the grozing iron and traced over the shape. When cold water was poured on the glass, it cracked along the marks of the hot iron. The glazier then used a notch at the other end of the grozing iron to chip away and smooth the rough edges.

The framework that held the quarries together was made up of strips of pliable lead known variously as cames or calms. On

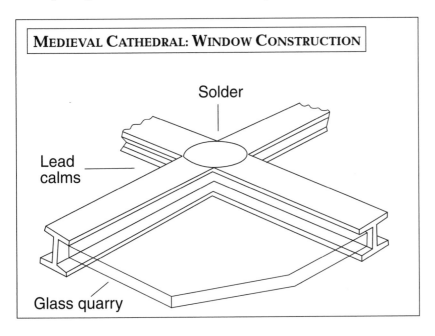

MEDIEVAL CATHEDRAL: WINDOW CONSTRUCTION

Solder

Lead calms

Glass quarry

either side of these strips were grooves into which cement was placed. The individual pieces of glass were slipped into the grooves and the lead was pinched shut to secure them.

Solder made of lead and tin held the lead strips together, and strands of copper wire were soldered to the outsides of the frame. When the sections were lifted into place, the copper wires were wound tightly to the adjoining section and eventually around the mullion bars to hold the structure in place.

LARGER WINDOWS

As the masons and glaziers improved their skills, windows grew ever larger. The great west window at York Minster in England is more than fifty feet high. The church of Sainte-Chapelle, adjacent to the cathedral of Notre Dame in Paris, features sixteen windows picturing 1,134 biblical scenes.

The awe-inspiring windows of Sainte-Chappelle depict 1,134 biblical scenes and shower the church with heavenly light when sun shines through them.

ROSE WINDOWS

The most popular and most frequently found type of window built in medieval cathedrals was the rose window, a large round construction. While some small round windows with stained glass were occasionally found in Romanesque churches, it was Abbot Suger who first made the round window a major design element in his abbey church of Saint-Denis in the 1100s.

Most churches were built on an east-west orientation, with the altar at the west end and the front doors facing eastward toward Jerusalem. Suger's design called for a large round window to be placed where it would catch the rays of the rising sun and diffuse them through colored glass into the nave.

Suger's vision inspired copies throughout France and then throughout the rest of Europe. The basic design called for radiating forms, or petals, each tipped by a pointed arch. In the center was a circle of stone filled with tracery.

The rose window on the west front of Notre Dame at Chartres.

The development of iron mullion bars enabled rose windows to grow larger as the Middle Ages progressed. One of the largest and most impressive dominates the west front of Notre Dame at Chartres and measures thirty-nine feet in diameter.

When sunlight poured through these multicolored windows, it was, indeed, like beams from heaven. It was not the harsh, unfiltered daylight of the outside world but rather a radiant sparkle, as if the windows were filled with an array of jewels. The glittering display was not constant, varying with the position and brightness of the sun.

The earliest medieval stained glass windows consisted primarily of geometric patterns. Later, glass was used to make pictures, such as scenes from the Bible or portraits of kings or saints. As artists sought to make the scenes more lifelike, they began to devise and use techniques of painting on glass.

Wall paintings, such as this one showing Saint Paul shaking off a viper, decorated the interior of medieval cathedrals.

PAINTED GLASS

At first, paint was used only to add detail—a fold of a robe or lines in a face. Gradually, however, painted glass began to replace stained glass. Pot-metal glass was ground fine and mixed with animal fat to make a paint that was applied to the glass and then baked in a kiln to fix. The problem was that the glass in the paint and the glass under it were of different consistencies. Over time, paint began to flake and the windows either were allowed to deteriorate or had to be replaced.

When ways were found to make larger panes, glass became virtually an artist's canvas rather than a medium in itself. Windows grew brighter, and scenes became more realistic. The soft, peaceful charm of the old stained glass windows was abandoned in favor of a more vibrant reality. As historian Sartell Prentice writes,

> Instead of helping him [the worshiper] to forget the world the windows called him forth; here he saw, in perspective, the same [world] from which he had sought escape when he passed through the portals of the church. The restfulness of the old was gone, and in its place was only the suggestion of action, of stir and bustle, or noise and triumph.[19]

WALL DECORATION

The walls of medieval cathedrals, however, were not entirely windows and glass. There still were large expanses of stone. In the Middle Ages, these walls would have been highly decorated, painted with murals and draped with colorful tapestries. Visitors today, however, see these walls mostly in their unadorned state, the murals and tapestries having faded, disintegrated or been destroyed by zealous reformers.

When the walls were finished, plasterers covered them with a smooth surface, ready for painting. Most wall paintings were murals showing biblical scenes. Painters ground their own pigments and made brushes out of the bristle from hogs or badgers or from the hair of squirrels. Gold leaf—gold hammered into paper-thin leaves—was used extensively, especially on the haloes of saints. These murals, with the gold leaf shimmering in the light from the stained glass windows, must have truly made the cathedral interior the vision of heaven that the builders intended.

Medieval painters most often used a technique known as fresco, from the Italian word for "fresh." Pigments were mixed with egg yolks and were applied to plaster that was not quite dry. The paint combined with the moist plaster and the result, when dry, was a rich, vibrant color. Some surviving cathedral frescoes, once the grime of centuries has been painstakingly cleaned away, are as bright as they were when new.

Painting was not limited to the walls. Plaster also frequently covered the vaulted ceilings. In some cathedrals, workers painted lines to simulate the stones of the vault, making each one appear the same size to give the webbing an appearance of perfection when viewed from below. In others, however, painters continued to portray an earthly vision of heaven, filling the towering vaults with suns, moons, and shining gold-leaf stars.

TAPESTRIES

Tapestries and other wall hangings were popular. Not only were they beautiful and instructive, many showing stories from the Bible, but they were also functional. Medieval stone churches,

The Bayeux Tapestry, made by nuns in France, tells the story of William the Conqueror's invasion of England.

no matter how well constructed, were drafty, and hangings served to keep the cold wind from seeping in.

Tapestries were usually made by groups of nuns and were then given to cathedrals. Like the painters, they spared no expense, using yards of gold thread and weaving precious jewels into the pattern. The most famous medieval wall hanging is the Bayeux Tapestry, made by English nuns in France to tell the story of William the Conqueror's invasion of England. Although not technically a tapestry since the picture was embroidered onto linen rather than being woven into the pattern, the work was so fine that William himself said, "The women of England are very skillful with the needle."[20] Of course, the subject matter may have influenced his judgment.

STATUARY

Statuary was an important part of medieval cathedral decoration. Every projection of stone—corbels, gargoyles, bosses—was fertile ground for the freestone carvers who filled them with floral patterns, monsters, angels, and even scenes from everyday life. At Notre Dame in Paris a series of relief carvings depicts the four seasons, winter being shown as a peasant carrying a load of firewood. Sometimes carvings pictured silversmiths or other craftsmen at work. These might well have been donated and paid for by the guilds represented, as was frequently the case with stained glass windows.

A relief carving from the right door of Chartres Cathedral's west facade.

Most cathedral statuary and carvings were on the exterior. Major exceptions included the choir and the great screens separating the nave from the choir and the altar from the shrines behind it. The screen between the nave and choir was called the jubé in France and the rood screen in England because it was usually topped with a cross, or rood. The screen separating the altar and shrines was called the reredos. Use of these screens grew in the later Middle Ages, and they were covered with elaborate carvings. The rood screen at York Minster is a mixture of wood and stone with recesses for fifteen larger-than-life statues of kings of England.

Statuary was even more elaborate on cathedral exteriors. Two of the best examples are at Reims and Amiens in France. The west facades abound with representations of Jesus' apostles, Old Testament prophets, and saints. Piers and buttresses are covered with relief carvings depicting biblical scenes.

The elaborately carved rood screen at York Minster.

THE TYMPANA

The key exterior carving was done over the three great main doors to the cathedral, the porta ceili, or "gateways to heaven." Over each door was a tympanum, a semicircular panel crowded with relief carvings. These carvings, like stained glass windows and tracery, were first sketched out on the tracing room floor. Masons then cut flat pieces of freestone—most of them larger than a person and some much larger—to the exact shapes that would be used in the tympanum. Designs were traced onto the stones and were then carved into them. When the carvings were finished, the individual stones were lifted and mortared into place.

One of the most outstanding sets of doorways is found at Notre Dame in Paris. The cathedral's portals, writes historian Ann Mitchell, display "the whole philosophy of the age." [21] The theme of the center tympanum is the Last Judgment, with the central figure of Jesus, majestic and powerful and also compassionate. Angels flutter at his shoulders while below, those whom he has judged are separated into the blessed and the damned. The tympana above the doors on either side both picture the Virgin Mary, patron saint of the cathedral.

FLOOR DECORATION

Every surface of a cathedral was used for symbolic decoration, and the floor was no exception. There were no pews or benches, as in

Scenes from the Last Judgment adorn the tympana at Paris's Notre Dame Cathedral.

modern churches; worshipers either stood or knelt. Some English cathedrals employed black-and-white checkerboard patterns throughout the vast expanses of the nave, emblematic of the struggle between good and evil. The much more popular motif was a huge maze composed of tile or marble that was a different color than the rest of the floor. The maze was symbolic of a person's journey through the twists and turns of earthly life before reaching heaven. Pilgrims who found their way to the center of the maze were considered to have received God's blessing.

Wood, having played important but lackluster roles as supports, scaffolding, and roof beams in the basic construction of the cathedral, played a major part in the decoration. Many choir screens were made of wood. The stalls where the individual monks of the chapter sat inside the choir were of highly detailed wood carving. The bishop's throne was usually carved and covered with gold leaf, and the pulpit from which he gave his sermon was also wooden and covered with a canopy of the most delicate wooden tracery.

Doors throughout the cathedral were wooden, and they were often inlaid, carved, and richly painted, as were their frames. The huge outer doors, some as tall as twenty-five feet, were made of wooden planks held together with iron bands.

METALWORK

Metalworkers found plenty to do in the finishing of cathedrals. Brass was used for locks and for some hinges. Bronze was the favorite metal for bells, which were cast from molds made of clay and plaster. Cathedral bells were enormously heavy, and one of the most frequent and most destructive mishaps occurred when towers or spires caught fire and bells broke free to crash down through the ceiling.

Precious metals were used in abundance, probably more abundantly than the austere Bernard of Clairvaux would have liked. However, Bernard's contemporary, Suger of Saint-Denis, argued that service to God ought to be conducted "with all inner purity and with all outward splendor."[22] As a result of his influence, gold crosses set with gemstones adorned the altar. Communion was taken from silver plates and from jeweled silver and gold cups.

CONSECRATION

When a cathedral was completed, the bishop and the canons of the chapter conducted a service of consecration and thanksgiving. On the appointed day, the entire city trooped through the streets—the bishop first, followed by the canons and other clergy. Then came the nobility—perhaps even the king—and the common people last of all.

Ascending the stairs to the central door, the bishop rapped three times with his staff of office and cried out the biblical verse: "Lift up your heads, O ye gates, and be ye lifted up, ye everlasting doors, and the King of Glory shall come in." From inside, a voice asked, "Who is the King of Glory?" This was the signal for the multitude to shout with one voice, "The Lord of Hosts, he is the King of Glory!" At this, the doors opened wide and the bishop led his flock into the cathedral.

In most cases many years had passed since the building had been started. Few, if any, people at a consecration had been alive when the first stone of the foundation was laid. Workers in the congregation gazed about them, taking well-deserved pride in

A bell from the south tower of Notre Dame in Paris.

their accomplishments. Chances were they had used the skills and tools handed down to them by parents and grandparents.

As they stood, light spilling through the multicolored windows and glinting off the gold cross on the altar, they must have been almost overcome with awe. They must have had much the same experience as German poet Johann Wolfgang von Goethe, who wrote about his first sight of Strasbourg Cathedral:

> A sensation of wholeness and greatness filled my soul; which, composed of a thousand harmonious details, I could savour and enjoy, yet by no means understand or explain. So it is, men say, with the bliss of Heaven. . . . The cathedral rises like a sublime wide-arching Tree of God, that, with a thousand boughs, a million twigs, and leafage like the sands of the sea, proclaims the glory of the Lord.[23]

EPILOGUE

The age that gave birth to Gothic cathedrals was one of optimism, piety, religious zeal, and buoyant spirits. When that age died, Gothic architecture quickly withered, like a flower whose stem has been severed. There was a brief, final blooming, but the blossoms—though colorful—had lost their simple beauty. Eventually the medieval world gave way to an entirely new age: the Renaissance.

Throughout the 1300s the age that had been ushered in by the end of the first millennium was buffeted by forces that undermined the foundations on which the medieval spirit was built, particularly the innate goodness of humanity as creatures of God, the moral authority of the church, and the surety of God's mercy. These forces included the philosophy of Scholasticism, corruption within the church, the devastation of the Hundred Years' War between England and France, and the horrors of the Black Death.

Scholasticism emerged from a renewed interest in the study of the philosophy of the ancient Greeks. The Scholastics sought to explain as much as possible in terms of reason instead of faith. Thus, traditional teachings came under attack. Moral values, instead of being absolute, became subject to debate.

CHURCH CORRUPTION

The common people had little contact with Scholasticism, but they could readily see the decay within the church. Throughout the 1100s and 1200s many church leaders—popes, cardinals, and bishops—had become less servants of God than princes of men. They lived in lavish splendor, some openly with their mistresses and illegitimate children. They counseled kings on political rather than spiritual matters, putting national affairs before moral obligations.

Finally, in 1309, the papacy came entirely under secular control and was moved by the king of France from Rome to Avignon. It returned to Italy in 1377 only to fall into such disarray that there were sometimes two and even three rival popes. As historian Arthur Kingsley Porter writes,

> Never . . . had the Christian religion been so openly the object of scorn and derision. The Papacy lost both moral and political power . . . the clergy obeyed no discipline . . . monks and priests vied with each other in corruption.[24]

And, along with power, the church lost the trust and respect of the people.

THE HUNDRED YEARS' WAR

Of much more immediate concern to the people of France than the state of the church was the prospect that their homes would be destroyed and they and their families slaughtered. In 1339 rivalry between France and England in Flanders touched off a war that was to continue intermittently until 1453 and become known as the Hundred Years' War. Huge portions of France became battleground over which armies marched back and forth, killing and pillaging as they went.

When the armies departed, they were replaced by bands of armed outlaws from whom no one was safe. These bandits would ravage a district and move on, leaving desolation in their wake. The Italian poet Petrarch, upon visiting France, wrote,

The death and suffering caused by the Black Death weakened the foundations on which the medieval spirit was founded.

The English army besieges Calais during the Hundred Years' War, a war that destroyed much of France and shook the people's faith.

"Nothing presented itself to my eyes but a fearful solitude, an utter poverty, land uncultivated, houses in ruins." [25] The people's faith was shaken, both in the nature of their fellow humans and in the power of God to protect them.

THE BLACK DEATH

Their faith was shaken even more by the Black Death, a plague that swept across Europe between 1349 and 1351. As terrible as banditry was, it was at least somewhat understandable. However, there was no explaining the Black Death, which struck down rich and poor, saint and sinner. Somewhere between a quarter and a third of the people of western Europe perished, and as the death toll mounted, normal human relationships broke down. Husbands deserted wives; mothers abandoned their children. Many people, when their prayers for deliverance went unanswered, turned to lawlessness and immorality, reasoning that if God had lost the power to save, he had also lost the power to punish.

THE EFFECTS ON ARCHITECTURE

These societal upheavals came to be reflected in church architecture. Just as traditional values and teachings came under increasing challenge, builders forsook the traditional Gothic forms. Once carefully proportioned and built to impart a sense of harmony, cathedrals now mirrored the uncertainty of the times. Excesses became the rule rather than the exception.

Architects of cathedrals in the 1300s first became fascinated with height. Loftiness had always been a goal of designers, but the new style sacrificed horizontal and vertical proportion in favor of the long unbroken vertical line, abandoning the triforium and the clerestory gallery. The new style was called Perpendicular in England and Rayonnant in France, after the word *rayon*, French referring to a wheel spoke and originally applied to the long straight rose window mullions.

Compared to Gothic designs, the Perpendicular style seemed clean and precise yet cold and unemotional. Architectural historian Baring Gould calls it "a style that lent itself to be employed by second or third rate architects. The compass nipped genius. Any dull man . . . could design [a cathedral] which would be perfectly correct, and show no spark of invention."[26]

This rose window from Amiens in France is decorated with interwoven mullions, a common feature of the Flamboyant style.

FLAMBOYANT

In the last half of the 1300s cathedral design swung completely in the opposite direction. The austerity of the Perpendicular style gave way to a profusion of decoration. As with Rayonnant, this style, in France, took its name from an aspect of the rose window. Mullions, instead of projecting in straight lines from the center, curved in an interwoven pattern that, when filled with bright glass, resembled a flame. The new style came to be called Flamboyant. Across the channel in England it was known as Decorated.

In Flamboyant cathedrals, writes historian Sartell Prentice, "the Gothic church was a mere blank page upon which [the architect] might write, [covering] every available blank space. . . . He treated his stone like thread and wove patterns of lace upon the walls."[27] Vault ribs, once used sparingly and as supports, expanded into elaborate geometrical patterns. Where piers met the ceiling, they erupted into ribs that spread outward like the spokes of an umbrella in what was known as fan vaulting.

On the outside, tracery covered almost all surfaces like lacework made of stone. Statues filled every niche. Pinnacles and spires had so many finials that one critic complained that they resembled quills upon a fretful porcupine. The Flamboyant style was an exhibition of how skillful the medieval worker had become, but the effect was one of gaudiness. It was as if the designers, unable to find new decorative ideas, simply multiplied the old ones as many times as possible.

Some experts have claimed that Flamboyant cathedral architecture was a joyful reaction to a long truce in the Hundred Years' War and to the disappearance—temporarily—of the Black Death. Just the opposite is possible, however. The desperate, almost frantic fervor displayed by survivors of the plague may have spread to architects. There is uncertainty under the exuberance; the liveliness is forced and strained. As Prentice writes, "Behind these leaping, flame-like mullions there is no leaping of the heart; in these slender window-bars of stone that now advance and then retreat, you seem to hear the crackling of skeleton castanets."[28]

THE RENAISSANCE

Gothic cathedrals, along with their Rayonnant and Flamboyant permutations, were soon to become only echoes. Starting in Italy in about 1400, new ideas, built on the classical ages of Greece and Rome, began to dominate art and architecture. This return to classicism was called the Renaissance, or "rebirth." Architects began to retreat from the styles of the last 250 years. The barrel vaults and heavy walls of the Romanesque style reappeared. Eventually cathedrals were being built in exactly the same manner in which they had originated—the basilica.

Subsequent centuries were not kind to medieval cathedrals. They were considered crude and ugly by Renaissance standards. Murals were painted over; tapestries were allowed to disintegrate. Stained glass windows were replaced with clear glass, yielding more light but less beauty.

AMERICAN GOTHIC

While many Gothic cathedrals in Europe have been preserved or restored to their original splendor, one does not have to travel to Europe to see an example of a true Gothic cathedral—one is located near Washington, D.C.

Officially the Cathedral Church of Saint Peter and Saint Paul, it is better known as the Washington National Cathedral. It was originally proposed by Pierre L'Enfant when he drew up his plan for the city, but not until 1907 was the foundation stone laid at the fifty-seven-acre site on St. Alban's Hill, the city's highest point.

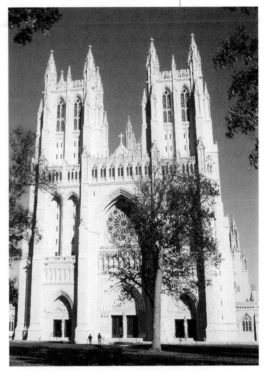

Although the Washington National Cathedral was built using modern tools, the design and construction process are the same as in the Middle Ages. Stone is mortared on stone with no reliance on structural steel. Masons labored on scaffolding, carving delicate statues much as their ancestors might have done.

Indeed, the work lasted as long as on a medieval cathedral. It sometimes lagged for lack of funds, but it never entirely stopped. The great central tower was completed in 1964, and on September 29, 1990, the final stone was put into place on the southwest tower.

The Washington National Cathedral, built in the Gothic style, ranks as the sixth largest cathedral in the world.

The cathedral, at a length of 514 feet, is the sixth-largest in the world. It contains 200 stained glass windows, the glass for which was made using the traditional pot-metal technique. The great rose window alone contains 10,500 pieces of glass and depicts scenes from the Book of Genesis in the Bible.

Built in the twentieth century, the Guildford Cathedral in England stands as proof that the Gothic spirit has not died.

The cathedrals suffered more indignities during the Protestant Reformation. In their zeal to destroy any remnants of Catholicism, Protestants smashed altar rails and screens and sang hymns around the bonfires made from their remnants. Statues were pulled down and broken up. Much of the stained glass that had survived the Renaissance fell before the hammers of reformers.

The Gothic spirit, however, was not dead, only diminished. It flared anew in the 1800s in what was called the Gothic Revival. Ancient cathedrals were restored to their former glory. New cathedrals, such as those at Guildford and Liverpool in England, were built in the Gothic style. The revival awoke echoes of a distant past and of the spirit in which these mighty works were built and dedicated to God. It recalled the words of Abbot Suger, carved on the west doors of his mighty church at Saint-Denis:

> Glory not at the gold and the costs, but at the work that is in this feat! Noble is the work, but the work which shines here so nobly should lighten the hearts so that, through true lights, they can reach the one true light, where Christ is the true door. . . . The dull spirit rises up through the material to the truth, and although he was cast down before, he arises new when he has seen this light. [29]

NOTES

Chapter 1: The Christian Heritage

1. Quoted in Jeannette Mirsky, *Houses of God*. New York: Viking, 1965, p. 136.
2. Quoted in Sartell Prentice, *The Heritage of the Cathedral*. New York: William Morrow, 1936, p. 40.
3. Quoted in Wim Swaan, *The Gothic Cathedral*. New York: Doubleday, 1969, p. 23.
4. Prentice, *The Heritage of the Cathedral,* p. 111.

Chapter 2: The Gothic Vision

5. Quoted in Otto von Simson, *The Gothic Cathedral*. New York: Pantheon Books, 1956, p. 52.
6. Von Simson, *The Gothic Cathedral*, p. 53.
7. Quoted in von Simson, *The Gothic Cathedral*, p. 100.
8. Quoted in Jean Gimpel, *The Cathedral Builders*. New York: Grove, 1961, p. 26.

Chapter 3: The Builders

9. Quoted in Gimpel, *The Cathedral Builders*, p. 165.
10. Gimpel, *The Cathedral Builders*, p. 66.
11. Quoted in Gunther Binding, *High Gothic: The Age of Great Cathedrals*. Cologne, Germany: Taschen, 1999, p. 65.
12. Quoted in Gimpel, *The Cathedral Builders*, p. 135.
13. Quoted in Gimpel, *The Cathedral Builders*, p. 75.
14. Quoted in Gimpel, *The Cathedral Builders*, p. 135.

Chapter 4: Raising the Walls

15. Quoted in Swaan, *The Gothic Cathedral*, p. 48.

Chapter 5: Roof and Ceiling

16. John Fitchen, *The Construction of Gothic Cathedrals*. London: Oxford University Press, 1961, p. 29.

Chapter 6: The Word Made Flesh

17. Quoted in Fiona Macdonald and John James, *Medieval Cathedral*. New York: Peter Bedrick Books, 1991, p. 26.
18. Gimpel, *The Cathedral Builders*, p. 95.
19. Prentice, *The Heritage of the Cathedral*, p. 178.
20. Quoted in Macdonald and James, *Medieval Cathedral*, p. 30.
21. Ann Mitchell, *Cathedrals of Europe*. Feltham, England: Hamlyn, 1968, p. 63.

22. Quoted in Swaan, *The Gothic Cathedral*, p. 55.

23. Quoted in Swaan, *The Gothic Cathedral*, p. 101.

Epilogue

24. Quoted in Prentice, *The Heritage of the Cathedral*, p. 127.

25. Quoted in Prentice, *The Heritage of the Cathedral*, p. 195.

26. Quoted in Prentice, *The Heritage of the Cathedral*, p. 202.

27. Prentice, *The Heritage of the Cathedral*, p. 207.

28. Prentice, *The Heritage of the Cathedral*, p. 210.

29. Quoted in Binding, *High Gothic*, p. 44.

Glossary

altar: A raised platform, normally located over the crypt, on which the communion service is conducted.

ambulatory: A curved walkway around the apse and behind the altar.

apse: The semicircular recess to the rear of the altar.

arcade: A line of arches, raised on pillars or columns, forming the lower part of the wall surrounding the apse and the choir.

atrium: An open area in front of the cathedral; originally a place where the unbaptized could receive instruction.

barrel vault: A simple vault of semicircular construction with no cross vaults.

basillica: The Roman law court whose style was copied in early Christian churches.

batten: Wooden rafters over which roofing material was placed.

buttress: A projecting or freestanding pillar on the exterior wall that takes up the lateral strain from the ceiling and roof.

came: A grooved strip of lead designed to hold pieces of stained glass in place.

canon: A priest belonging to the staff of a cathedral.

cathedra: Latin for the throne used by the bishop of a cathedral.

centering: A large type of wooden falsework, or framing, on which stone arches were constructed.

chancel: The area of a cathedral encompassing the apse, altar, and choir.

chapter: The body of priests, or canons, on a cathedral staff; the word derives from the reading of a chapter from the writings of St. Benedict at each meeting.

choir: The area between the altar and the congregation; usually has seats along each side for singers.

clerestory: The highest of the three levels of the main cathedral wall; consists primarily of stained glass windows in Gothic churches.

cloister: An enclosed area, developed from the atrium, where the clergy can walk and meditate.

corbel: A weight-bearing projection, either of stone or wood, from a wall.

crypt: An underground chamber, usually below the altar, used for burials.

dean: The chief officer of the chapter.

Decorated: A highly ornamental version of later Gothic churches; known in France as Flamboyant.

falsework: A wooden framing on which stone arches were constructed.

finial: A decorative stone projection on a spire.

flashing: Lead sheets used to waterproof the intersection of a wall and the roof; also a method of coloring stained glass by fusing glass of two colors.

flying buttress: An arch, rising at an angle from a freestanding pillar, that takes the lateral thrust of the roof and ceiling.

freestone mason: Carvers of delicate stonework, such as tracery, gargoyles, and statues.

fresco: A type of mural painting in which colors are applied to damp plaster.

gargoyle: A decorative, often highly fanciful, stone waterspout projecting from a roof.

glazier: a glassworker.

Gothic: The name, originally derogatory, given to the type of large churches built in western Europe between about 1050 and 1250.

groin vault: The intersection of two barrel vaults of the same height.

grozing: The cutting of glass with a heated iron.

lagging: Lightweight curved boards placed between the ribs of a vault to serve as a platform for stones of webbing.

mortise-tenon: The system of fastening beams together by inserting wooden tongues into corresponding notches.

mullion: Iron bars diving large windows.

narthex: A foyer, or lobby, between the front door and the nave.

nave: The main part of a church, usually divided by aisles, set aside for the congregation.

Perpendicular: A very severe, precise style of later-Gothic church architecture; known in France as Rayonnant.

pinnacle: A narrow, pointed tower atop a pier or buttress; used both as a decoration and to add weight.

quarry: A place where stone is excavated; also, in glass-work, the individual pieces of stained glass that make up a window.

reredos: An ornamental wooden or stone screen behind the altar.

rib: A stone arch rising from piers and spanning part of a vault.

Romanesque: The style of church architecture preceding Gothic; characterized by the use of round arches and massive walls.

rood screen: A wooden or stone screen, often topped by a cruci-fix, between the choir and the nave.

rose window: A large round stained glass window whose pan-els, radiating from the center, resemble petals; usually found above the center front door.

roughstone mason: Workers who shaped and laid the larger stones as opposed to the freestone masons who did the more delicate carving.

tie beam: The large wooden beam extending transversely across sets of piers to form the base of the roof truss.

tracery: The geometrically constructed stonework used to fill in windows and arches.

transept: A secondary nave built at a right angle to the main nave; normally built in pairs to form a cross with the main body of the church.

triforium: A section of the main wall between the arcade and the clerestory; occasionally contained a passage above the arcade.

truss: Beams connected to form a rigid framework for the roof.

tympana: Panels, normally semicircular, located above a main door and filled with carvings, usually of biblical scenes.

vault: A curved, self-supporting wall surface resting on pillars or piers and covering a space.

voussoir: One of the wedge-shaped stones making up an arch.

webbing: Bricks or small stones laid between ribs to make up the largest sections of a vault.

WORKS CONSULTED

David Aldred, *Castles and Cathedrals*. Cambridge, England: Cambridge University Press, 1993. A short, interesting description of the roles of castles and cathedrals in medieval Europe.

Gunther Binding, *High Gothic: The Age of Great Cathedrals*. Cologne, Germany: Taschen, 1999. A well-written and superbly photographed account of the development of Gothic churches.

Giovanni Caselli, *The Middle Ages*. New York: Peter Bedrick Books, 1988. A simply written and well-illustrated account of life in medieval Europe.

Flavio Conti, *Splendor of the Gods*. Boston: Harcourt Brace Jovanovich, 1978. Contains color pictures and well-illustrated text describing some of the world's most outstanding places of worship.

Lynn T. Courtenay, ed., *The Engineering of Medieval Cathedrals*. Aldershot, England: Ashgate, 1977. A highly technical book with chapters by various experts dealing with different aspects of cathedral building.

D. H. S. Cranage, *Cathedrals and How They Were Built*. Cambridge, England: Cambridge University Press, 1948. Concentrates on English cathedrals and is especially good at describing medieval foundations.

John Fitchen, *The Construction of Gothic Cathedrals*. London: Oxford University Press, 1961. An extremely technical description, written by a professor of architecture, of how vaults of medieval cathedrals were built.

Jean Gimpel, *The Cathedral Builders*. New York: Grove, 1961. An extremely comprehensive account of the people who built the medieval cathedrals, examining the different crafts and professions.

Fiona Macdonald and John James, *Medieval Cathedral*. New York: Peter Bedrick Books, 1991. For younger readers this is an excellent, lavishly illustrated description of cathedrals and their construction.

Jeannette Mirsky, *Houses of God*. New York: Viking, 1965. An account of the development of houses of worship of the world's major religions.

Ann Mitchell, *Cathedrals of Europe*. Feltham, England: Hamlyn, 1968. A good overall summary of cathedral building plus a comprehensive look at twelve of Europe's best-known cathedrals.

Helen Huss Parkhurst, *Cathedral: A Gothic Pilgrimage*. Boston: Houghton Mifflin, 1936. A classic account of the cathedral as the focus of medieval life and the reflection of medieval thought.

Sartell Prentice, *The Heritage of the Cathedral*. New York: William Morrow, 1936. An elegantly written examination of the influence of history on cathedral architecture.

Otto von Simson, *The Gothic Cathedral*. New York: Pantheon Books, 1956. An in-depth look at the origins of Gothic architecture and its reflection of the medieval mind.

Wim Swaan, *The Gothic Cathedral*. New York: Doubleday, 1969. A highly readable and comprehensive examination of Gothic architecture explaining the cathedral's role in society.

Percy Watson, *Building the Medieval Cathedrals*. Cambridge, England: Cambridge University Press, 1976. A small but very informative and well-illustrated account of how cathedrals were built.

INDEX

PICTURE CREDITS

ABOUT THE AUTHOR

William W. Lace is a native of Fort Worth, Texas. He holds a bachelor's degree from Texas Christian University, a master's from East Texas State University, and a doctorate from the University of North Texas. After working for newspapers in Baytown, Texas, and Fort Worth, he joined the University of Texas at Arlington as sports information director and later became the director of the news service. He is now executive assistant to the chancellor for the Tarrant County College District in Fort Worth. He and his wife, Laura, live in Arlington and have two children. Lace has written numerous other works for Lucent Books, one of which—*The Death Camps* in the Holocaust Library series—was selected by the New York Public Library for its 1999 Recommended Teenage Reading List.